The New Pathway to Summit

Students' Workbook

Einführungsphase Sekundarstufe II

Herausgegeben von:
Iris Edelbrock

Erarbeitet von:
Iris Edelbrock und Birgit Schmidt-Grob

Sprachliche Betreuung:
Elin Arbin unter Mitarbeit von Samantha Hooton

Schöningh

Die Begleitmaterialien zu "The New Pathway" können über den Buchhandel oder direkt beim Verlag bezogen werden:

The New Pathway Students' Book
Best.-Nr. 040032

The New Pathway Audio-CD mit Hörtexten und Songs
Best-Nr. 062416

The New Pathway Exam Trainer
Best.-Nr. 062444-2

www.schoeningh-schulbuch.de
Schöningh Verlag, Jühenplatz 1–3, 33098 Paderborn

Druck 5 4 3 2 1 / Jahr 2014 13 12 11 10
Die letzte Zahl bezeichnet das Jahr dieses Druckes.

Umschlaggestaltung: Nora Krull, Bielefeld
Druck und Bindung: westermann Druck GmbH, Braunschweig

ISBN 978-3-14-040034-3

Contents

Listening comprehension tasks; listening to a song/text/speech/interview

Task with reference to film viewing/the interactive CD-ROM

The answer to this exercise should be written in the exercise book or on a sheet of paper.

Nature & Environment: Go Green – Save the Earth?!

School's Out – What Next? How to Make Your Life Meaningful ...

Minorities in Great Britain and the USA – Redefining Race and Multi-Ethnicity

Imagination and Images – Projects on Literature and Film

Pronunciation and Phonetic Symbols

Consonants

p	pen	/pen/
b	bad	/bæd/
t	tea	/tiː/
d	did	/dɪd/
k	cat	/kæt/
g	get	/get/
tʃ	chain	/tʃeɪn/
dʒ	jam	/dʒæm/
f	fall	/fɔːl/
v	van	/væn/
θ	thin	/θɪn/
ð	this	/ðɪs/

s	see	/siː/
z	zoo	/zuː/
ʃ	shoe	/ʃuː/
ʒ	vision	/'vɪʒn/
h	hat	/hæt/
m	man	/mæn/
n	now	/naʊ/
ŋ	sing	/sɪŋ/
l	leg	/leg/
r	red	/red/
j	yes	/jes/
w	wet	/wet/

The symbol (r) indicates that British pronunciation will have /r/ only if a vowel sound follows directly at the beginning of the next word, as in **far away**; otherwise the /r/ is omitted. For American English, all the /r/ sounds should be pronounced.

/x/ represents a fricative sound as in /lɒx/ for Scottish **loch**, Irish **louth**.

Stress

The mark /'/ shows the main stress in a word. Compare **able** /'eɪbl/, stressed on the first syllable, with **ability** /ə'bɪləti/, stressed on the second. A stressed syllable is relatively loud, long in duration, said clearly and distinctly, and made noticeable by the pitch of the voice.

Longer words may have one or more secondary stresses coming before the main stress. These are marked with /ˌ/ as in **abbreviation** /əˌbriːvi'eɪʃn/, **agricultural** /ˌægrɪ'kʌltʃərəl/. They feel like beats in a rhythm leading up to the main stress.

Weak stresses coming after the main stress in a word can sometimes be heard, but they are not marked in this dictionary.

When two words are together in a phrase, the main stress in the first word may shift to the place of the secondary stress to avoid a clash between two stressed syllables next to each other. For instance, **ˌafter'noon** has the main stress on **noon**, but in the phrase **ˌafternoon 'tea** the stress on noon is missing. **ˌWell 'known** has the main stress on **known**, but in the phrase **ˌwell-known 'actor** the stress on **known** is missing.

Vowels and diphthongs

iː	see	/siː/	
i	happy	/'hæpi/	
ɪ	sit	/sɪt/	
e	ten	/ten/	
æ	cat	/kæt/	
ɑː	father	/'fɑːðə(r)/	
ɒ	got	/gɒt/	*(British English)*
ɔː	saw	/sɔː/	
ʊ	put	/pʊt/	
u	actual	/'æktʃuəl/	
uː	too	/tuː/	
ʌ	cup	/kʌp/	

ɜː	fur	/fɜː(r)/	
ə	about	/ə'baʊt/	
eɪ	say	/seɪ/	
əʊ	go	/gəʊ/	*(British English)*
oʊ	go	/goʊ/	*(American English)*
aɪ	my	/maɪ/	
ɔɪ	boy	/bɔɪ/	
aʊ	now	/naʊ/	
ɪə	near	/nɪə(r)/	*(British English)*
eə	hair	/heə(r)/	*(British English)*
ʊə	pure	/pjʊə(r)/	*(British English)*

Oxford Advanced Learner's Dictionary, 8th Edition, Oxford, Oxford University Press, 2010, pp. R 45 f.

Standardized Terminology for Tasks

The New Pathway, p. 8

COMPREHENSION
Vocab Training

a. Assign the terms and phrases to the respective tasks they are related to.

analysis and re-structuring of texts

orientation/comprehension/understanding/reproduction of texts

discussion/evaluation/text production

define comment (on) examine

outline discuss assess describe state

contrast illustrate point out justify

sum up evaluate compare prove

define reflect on interpret present

characterize summarize analyze

explain speculate on clarify imagine

write a characterization demonstrate

ACTIVITY
Writing Practice

b. You are the expert now:
Have a look at the textual and visual elements on pp. 10f. of your Students' Book and think up questions and tasks yourself. Be sure to match the respective terms and tasks appropriately.
Read out and compare your tasks in class.

Growing Up – Youth and Age in Modern Society

The New Pathway, p. 10

1 Teach Five-Year-Olds to Beware of Advertising

The following newspaper article reveals and criticizes that even five-year-old children are being (ab-) used by advertising slogans and commercial messages in order to "commercialize childhood".

COMPREHENSION

Reading Comprehension
→ FoS, Reading Techniques, p. 59

a. Collect the information given in the article and explain which techniques and tricks are being used to lure children to consume goods.

schools	playgrounds	at home	leisure time
• free samples • ...	• design based on TV characters • ...	• Internet/online marketing • ...	• rock concerts sponsored by beer firms • ...

ANALYSIS

Text Analysis
→ FoS, Analysis of a Non-Fictional Text, p. 96

b. Explain what, according to the article, can be done to teach children and teenagers to beware of advertising.

Companies Increasingly Try to Exploit Schools as Part of the Commercialization of Childhood

Children as young as five should be given lessons in how to deal with the onslaught of adverts hurled at them, a government inquiry has found. **(1)**
The inquiry into the commercialization of childhood revealed that firms spend at least £100bn each year advertising to children in the UK. **(2)** It said children are increasingly bombarded by brands, advertising slogans and commercial messages. **(3)** Even children in primary school need lessons in becoming media-savvy consumers, according to the inquiry by Prof. David Buckingham, an international expert on children's consumption of the web, TV and adverts. **(4)**
Companies increasingly use schools and playgrounds to conduct their market research, distribute free samples of their products and advertise their logos, the inquiry, commissioned by the Department for Children, Schools and Families, found. **(5)** Some companies offer schools free classroom exercise books that carry adverts from soft drink companies and pop bands, while others specialize in placing advertising posters in schools. **(6)** A growing number of schools are sponsored by or managed by firms. **(7)**
Companies such as Nestlé and Kellogg's sponsor school awards, while Tesco and Cadbury have encouraged pupils and their parents to collect tokens in exchange for computers and sports equipment. **(8)** [...]
Outside school, children are spending increasing amounts of time in branded leisure centres, Buckingham found. **(9)** Playgrounds have opened up based on TV characters and toys, such as Charlie Chalk. **(10)** Rock concerts for teenagers are sponsored by beer firms and have offered consumers limited edition bottles. **(11)**
Some online marketing techniques ask children to recommend products to their friends or target children who have bought certain products in the past, the inquiry found. **(12)**
"This raises some ethical concerns about potential deception and threats to privacy ... [...]", Buckingham said. **(13)** "While children can generally recognize the persuasive intentions of television advertising at a fairly young age, this is not necessarily the case with other forms of marketing and promotion ... used in new media." **(14)**
Buckingham said that pupils in primary and secondary schools needed lessons in "media literacy". **(15)**

Jessica Shepherd, guardian.co.uk, December 14, 2009 [07.04.2010]

c. Transform the sentences from passive into active voice or vice versa. Sometimes you have to change the sentence structure or you might have to find a suitable subject or by-agents.

Example: *Schools are increasingly (being) exploited by companies as part of the commercialization of childhood.*

GRAMMAR
Active and Passive Voice
→ Grammar Kit, p. 213

d. Choose from the list of verbs and nouns and find the appropriate synonyms for these verbs.

Synonyms
→ FoL, Improving Your Style, p. 130

to purchase   object   to like   to gain   article

to take pleasure in   to invest in   to take delight in

item   to get   to fancy   substance   to acquire

goods   product   merchandise   commodities   to bargain for

to enjoy

________ (1) ________ (2) ________ (3)

________ (4)

to buy

________ (5) ________ (6)

________ (7) ________ (8)

________ (9) ________ (10)

thing

________ (11) ________ (12) ________ (13)

________ (14) ________ (15) ________ (16)

________ (17) ________ (18)

e. Take a closer look at the girl and the boy in the middle of all their favourite things on pp. 10f. in your Students' Book again. Use your dictionary and find adjectives that describe the positive or negative emotions that might be connected with the children's situation.

ACTIVITY
Vocab Training

positive emotions	**negative emotions**
happy, pleased, ...	*overwhelmed, lonely, ...*
________	________
________	________
________	________
________	________
________	________

The New Pathway, p. 12

2 Temptations – Dreams or Nightmares?

After having discussed the various implications of tempting situations and/or things, you have gained an insight into the complexity of the problem.

COMPREHENSION
Taking Notes

a. Consider the positive and negative effects of 'temptations' that you have discussed in class and jot them down as shown in the grid below.

positive ...	negative effects of temptations
• *a feeling of satisfaction* • *a feeling of reward or consolation in stressful situations* • ...	• *not resisting temptations can lead to dependencies (consumption, drugs ...)* • ...

ACTIVITY
Writing Practice
→ FoS, Analysis of a Non-Fictional Text, p. 96

b. Use your mind map as well as your notes and write an argumentative text about 'Whether or what temptations should be resisted'.
Make sure that your text follows the **introduction – main part – conclusion pattern** and begins with a pithy (= *prägnant*) or provocative introductory sentence.

Example: *Shoplifting should not be considered a serious crime – don't all of us occasionally feel that urge to 'take a little something'? ... Why should we resist? ...*

The New Pathway, p. 15

3 Juno – Breaking the Big News

1, 2

Each scene in a film has been specifically composed to achieve an intended effect on the audience.

ANALYSIS
Reading for Detail
→ FoS, Analysis of Film Scene, p. 20

a. Reread the excerpt from the screenplay in your Students' Book on pp. 15 ff. and detect what hints are given about the function of the scene.

clues given concerning	lines	(possible) function of text passages and clues
the action		
creation of suspense	2–4 5–23	• *Bren and Mac are waiting for some bad news* • *Juno is under pressure/nervously pacing* • *parents make wrong guesses about Juno's problem* • ...
an unexpected turning-point		• ...
introduction of a (new) character	2–4	• *introduction of the characters* • ...
revealing a (new) character trait		• ...
relationships between characters		• ...

Film Analysis

b. Now, after having collected all the necessary information, write an analysis in which you explain the function of this scene.

c. The next day Leah reports the conversation to a mutual friend.
Use indirect speech. Be careful to employ different introductory verbs in order to give an account of the atmosphere and the (different) emotions of the people.

Here are some examples:
Juno hoped ... She explained ... Leah thought ... Mac pointed out ...
They disagreed ... Bren feared ... Mac expected ...

GRAMMAR
Indirect Speech
→ Grammar Kit, p. 215

4 Parents Hold the Key to Teenage Pregnancies: Broadsheet Versus Tabloid

The New Pathway p. 24

The following two texts are articles about Alfie Patten and his girlfriend Chantelle Steadman who became parents in February 2009. The articles are taken from different newspapers.

msnbc

British Boy Becomes Dad at 13

Baby-faced and only 4 feet tall, he was 12 when he impregnated girl, 14

LONDON. He's 13. He scarcely looks 10. And according to a British tabloid, he's a father.

Baby-faced and only 4 feet tall, the boy, Alfie Patten, was just 12 when he impregnated Chantelle, now 15, The Sun reported on Friday. Shown in a video posted Friday on the tabloid's website, the diminutive Alfie takes the newborn girl in his arms.

Asked what he would do to support the child financially, Alfie asks in a small, high-pitched voice, "What's financially?"

The girl was taking birth control pills but missed one, the newspaper reported. Friends and relatives left the family home near Eastbourne, about 70 miles southeast of London, on Friday without speaking to reporters gathered outside. The teenagers could not immediately be contacted.

The Sun did not say whether any tests were conducted to prove the boy's paternity. The paper did not offer any immediate comment when asked whether it had paid the family for the story.

Police and child services in Eastbourne, in southeast England, said in a statement that they were "aware of a 14-year-old girl that had become pregnant as the result of a relationship with a 12-year-old boy", adding that they were offering support to both young people.

Alfie's front page picture has sparked renewed debate about teen pregnancy in Britain. The country has one of the highest teen pregnancy rates in Europe, and government figures show that about 39,000 girls under the age of 18 became pregnant in 2006. More than 7,000 of those girls were younger than 16.

"I don't know the individual details of the case, but of course I think all of us would want to avoid teenage pregnancies," Prime Minister Gordon Brown said on Friday.

Britain had 27 births per 1,000 women aged 15–19 between 2000 and 2005, according to a report published by Population Action International. Comparable figures are 10 per 1,000 in Spain, 8 in 1,000 for France, and 5 in 1,000 for The Netherlands.

Britain's teen pregnancy rate, however, is still far below that of the United States, which registers 44 births per 1,000 women aged 15–19 and are more in line with English-speaking countries such as Australia and New Zealand, which respectively have 17 and 27 births per 1,000 women between 15 and 19, according to the report.

But the country's reputation as Europe's teen pregnancy capital has been an embarrassment to politicians.

In 1999 then-Prime Minister Tony Blair described Britain's record on pregnancies as shameful and vowed to turn it around.

"Put simply, you are still a child when you are 14 and, in a civilized society, children should not be having children," he said at the time. The government has since poured millions of pounds (dollars) into advertising and educational campaigns. [...]

Alfie's father, Dennis – who reportedly has nine children – said his son told him it was the first time he had had sex. He was reportedly allowed to sleep over at the girl's house.

The Associated Press, 2009; www.msnbc.msn.com/id/29184929 [27.03.2010]

THE Sun EXCLUSIVE

Baby-Faced Boy Alfie Patten is Father at 13

Boy dad Alfie Patten yesterday admitted he does not know how much nappies cost – but said: "I think it's a lot."

Baby-faced Alfie, who is 13 but looks more like eight, became a father four days ago when his girlfriend Chantelle Steadman gave birth to 7lb 3oz Maisie Roxanne.

He told how he and Chantelle, 15, decided against an abortion after discovering she was pregnant.

The shy lad, whose voice has not yet broken, said: "I thought it would be good to have a baby."

"I didn't think about how we would afford it. I don't really get pocket money. My dad sometimes gives me £10."

Alfie, who is just 4ft tall, added: "When my mum found out, I thought I was going to get in trouble. We wanted to have the baby but were worried how people would react."

"I didn't know what it would be like to be a dad. I will be good, though, and care for it."

Alfie's story, broken exclusively by The Sun today has sparked a huge politic storm with Tory leader David Cameron saying: "When I saw these pictures this morning, I just thought how worrying that in Britain today children are having children."

"I hope that somehow these children grow up into responsible parents but the truth is parenthood is just not something they should be thinking about right now." [...]

Maisie was conceived after Chantelle and Alfie – just 12 at the time – had a single night of unprotected sex.

They found out about the baby when Chantelle was 12 weeks pregnant.

But they kept it a secret until six weeks later when Chantelle's mum Penny, 38, became suspicious about her weight gain and confronted her.

After that Alfie's family told only those closest to them for fear he would be "demonized" at school. [...]

Chantelle admitted she and Alfie – who are both being supported by their parents – would be accused of being grossly irresponsible. She said: "We know we made a mistake but I wouldn't change it now. We will be good loving parents."

"I have started a church course and I am going to do work experience helping other young mums."

"I'll be a great mum and Alfie will be a great dad." [...]

Chantelle and Maisie were released from hospital yesterday. They are living with Penny, Chantelle's jobless dad Steve, 43, and her five brothers in a rented council house in Eastbourne. The family live on benefits. Alfie, who lives on an estate across town with mum Nicola, 43, spends most of his time at the Steadmans' house.

He is allowed to stay overnight and even has a school uniform there so he can go straight to his classes in the morning. [...]

Dennis, who works for a vehicle recovery firm, described Alfie as "a typical 13-year-old boy".

He said: "He loves computer games, boxing and Manchester United". Dennis, who has fathered nine kids, told how he was "gobsmacked" when he discovered Alfie was to be a dad, too.

Lucy Hagan, February 13, 2009,
www.thesun.co.uk/sol/homepage/news/article2233878.ece [27.03.2010]

COMPREHENSION

Summary Writing
→ FoS, Writing, p. 129

a. Read the two newspaper articles and summarize the information given in no more than 150 words.

- Use the simple present whenever possible to make your text as factual as possible.
- Use indirect speech to report what the respective people said.
- Focus on the facts and leave out minor details.

b. In order to determine the quality of different newspaper formats you need to examine the details of each article and pay attention to certain characteristics. Complete the following grid.

ANALYSIS
Stylistic Devices
→ FoF, The Press, p. 27

characteristic elements	The SUN	MSNBC
factual information	• names, age (13/15) • pocket money (£10)	• names/age • place • renewed debate in Britain • numbers
people/sources quoted	• Alfie, Chantelle • Tory leader David Cameron	
syntactic structure	• often direct speech • one sentence per paragraph	• mostly indirect speech
emotive words	• baby-faced, shy lad	• scarcely looks 10 • embarrassment
choice of words/ stylistic devices		
visual elements	• photograph showing the couple and their baby Maisie	
layout	• columns • short paragraphs	
→ conclusion		• more objective

The New Pathway, p. 28

5 How to End the War Over Sex Ed

COMPREHENSION

Structuring a Text
→ FoS, Reading Techniques, p. 59

The magazine article on Students' Book, pp. 28 f. contains many technical terms and is rather long. Therefore, before you start writing a summary, you should either divide the text into paragraphs or use the paragraphs given in the text.

a. Then, briefly sketch out the basic information of each paragraph.

lines	basic information
2–10	Jewel Morris-Davis, 16, high school sophomore, African-American, quiet, first person in her family who is not pregnant → proud
11–16	5 years ago – different situation, ...
17–27	
28–41	
42–49	
50–64	
65–78	
79–95	
96–103	
104–113	sex ed is difficult because of different influences from parents, media, friends, need to go on fighting teenage pregnancy because of rising birthrates in 2007, ...
114–end	

Summary Writing
→ FoS, Writing, p. 129

b. Now, after having structured the article, write a summary of about 150–200 words.

ANALYSIS

Working with Visuals
→ FoS, Analysis of Visuals, p. 134

c. Sarah Palin was the Republican vice president candidate in the U.S. presidential election campaign of 2008, and is known for her conservative attitude and views on sex education and abortion.

Describe the cartoon mocking the conservative politician Sarah Palin and her then [in 2008] pregnant 17-year-old daughter and relate it to the article "How to End the War Over Sex Ed".

6 A High School Teacher Talks About Teenage Pregnancy 2

The New Pathway, p. 32

COMPREHENSION

Listening for Detail
→ FoS, Listening Comprehension, p. 117

a. Listen carefully to the interview with high school teacher Ms. Shultz again and say which of these statements are right or wrong.
Sometimes more than one answer can be chosen.

1. FACS (Family and Consumer Sciences) courses help teenagers
   - ☐ a) to have an abortion
   - ☐ b) to develop skills about nutrition, finances, child development and housing skills
2. Reasons for teenagers to (voluntarily) get pregnant are
   - ☐ a) the hope that the baby may change their life in a positive way
   - ☐ b) date rape
   - ☐ c) the correct use of contraception
3. Ms. Shultz explains that ...
   - ☐ a) teenage moms want to be loved by their baby
   - ☐ b) the girls had sex because the boys told them how wonderful they are
   - ☐ c) sometimes young mothers are beaten up by their mothers because they had sex
4. The teenage mothers can expect
   - ☐ a) no difficulties at all – their friends will love and support them
   - ☐ b) a lack of support and many financial problems
   - ☐ c) that sometimes even teachers don't offer support to teenage mothers
5. Ms. Shultz points out that ...
   - ☐ a) school can offer counseling, child care and employment skills
   - ☐ b) for a teen mom high school offers the best opportunities
   - ☐ c) some teachers are prejudiced against teen mothers

6. Other teenagers react ...
   - ☐ a) in a supportive and understanding way
   - ☐ b) negatively, and gossip about the pregnant girl
   - ☐ c) in a shocked manner, because they are against sex before marriage
7. Teenage mothers are
   - ☐ a) mostly of African-American ethnicity
   - ☐ b) from poor families
   - ☐ c) to be found in all social groups
8. Governmental aid and financial help is given by the
   - ☐ a) BABE (Beds and Bridges) program
   - ☐ b) WIC (Women, Infants and Children) program
   - ☐ c) SUGAR program that helps teen mothers
9. These are the most popular sex ed programs:
   - ☐ a) Abortion Only helps pregnant teenagers
   - ☐ b) PSI (postponing sexual involvement) wants teenagers to stay virgins
   - ☐ c) FACS courses are very popular at high schools and all students have to attend them
10. The teenage fathers ...
    - ☐ a) are usually not supportive
    - ☐ b) show off with their fatherhood
    - ☐ c) offer generous financial help to the mother because they love the baby

b. Use the information provided in the interview and write an argumentative text: 'Should (high) schools offer sex education or not?'

ACTIVITY

Writing Practice
→ FoS, Analysis of a Non-Fictional Text, p. 96

The New Pathway, p. 34

7 Owen Meany – Being Attractive to Girls 3

COMPREHENSION

Listening for Detail

→ FoS, Listening Comprehension, p. 117

Writing a characterization of a literary character requires collecting as much information as possible to complete the picture.

a. Listen to the text *Being Attractive to Girls* again and take notes about Owen Meany.
Pay attention to

- what the narrator says about Owen Meany (**direct characterization**),
- what Owen himself reveals about his character in the way he behaves, reacts to the narrator, thinks about certain people/aspects (**indirect characterization**).

Fill in your findings in the diagram below.

relationships:

- ____
- ____
- ____
- ____
- ____

personal data:

age ____
profession ____
family ____

- ____
- ____

Owen Meany

behaviour:

- ____
- ____
- ____
- ____
- ____

outward appearance:

body ____
face ____

- ____
- ____
- ____

attitudes/views:

- ____
- ____
- ____
- ____
- ____

ACTIVITY

Writing Practice

b. Use the information that you have collected and write a characterization of Owen Meany. Don't forget to relate your findings to the text by quoting and referring to specific lines. Begin your characterization with the general data about Owen Meany.

8 When Eating Eats You Up – Anorexia & Obesity

The New Pathway, p. 36

According to a recent study by the International Association for the Study of Obesity (IASO), about 75 % of men and about 59 % of women living in Germany are overweight or obese. This means that there are more obese people in Germany than in any other European country.
Here is a collection of *Food Rules* about how to eat healthily.

Avoid food products containing ingredients that a third-grader cannot pronounce.

Avoid food products that contain more than five ingredients.

Do all your eating at a table.

Pay more, eat less.

Cook.

Eat only foods that will eventually rot.

Avoid foods you see advertised on television.

Eat only foods that have been cooked by humans.

Eat all the junk food you want as long as you cook it yourself.

Spend as much time enjoying the meal as it took to prepare it.

Don't get your fuel from the same place your car does.

Avoid food products containing ingredients that no ordinary human would keep in the pantry.

Don't eat anything your great-grandmother wouldn't recognize as food.

If it came from a plant, eat it; if it was made in a plant, don't.

Get out of the supermarket whenever you can.

Michael Pollan: Food Rules, New York, Penguin, 2009, pp. 7 ff.

a. These food rules are written in imperatives. Change the recommendations given into more polite sentences using **modal auxiliaries**.

GRAMMAR
Modal Auxiliaries

must mustn't may should (not) ought to

need (not) could might

Example: You should avoid foods you see advertised on television.

b. Explain the benefits of the given rules and recommendations with regards to health, the environment, and expenses. Make a ranking.

ACTIVITIES
Writing Practice

c. Do some research in your local supermarket and compare the prices of canned food to the expenses you would have if you bought fresh fruit, vegetables or meat.
Compare and discuss your findings in class.

The New Pathway, p. 37

9 New (Role) Models?

Why Too Thin Isn't 'In'

Top fashion designer Karl Lagerfeld has issued a vitriolic attack on less-than-rake-thin women that almost sounded like Rush Limbaugh blasting left-wing Democrats.

Lagerfeld, 71, mocked the dominant German women's magazine, *Brigitte*, for its decision to start using normal-sized women, instead of stick-like models, and celebrating their achievements.

"These are fat mummies sitting with their bags of crisps in front of the television," Lagerfeld sneered. "No one wants to see round women."

Lagerfeld's comments may once have been considered mainstream. No longer. Now they're just tacky. Last week, in fact, fashion house Ralph Lauren was forced to apologize for doctoring an ad to make an already skinny model look even more superhumanly thin.

Let's hope that Lagerfeld's comments will help stir serious debate about just why the size 0 ideal needs to be made a thing of the past. The cultural "heroin chic" fixation, dating to the 1960s and supermodel Twiggy, is destructive for women in general and particularly so for the young and impressionable.

Need proof? Just listen in to last weekend's National Tween Girl Summit in Washington for 9- to 14-year-olds. It was designed to encourage a more healthy attitude toward weight. "Every single person here wonders whether they've got the right body or the right look", a body-image columnist for *Seventeen* magazine said at the summit. All too often, it undermines self-esteem and encourages eating disorders.

The Tween Girl Summit showed that a serious cultural shift is possible – with a little assistance. Others providing that help in the past few years have included Dove's Campaign for Real Beauty, which features women of different shapes and sizes; the Council of Fashion Designers of America, which two years ago issued voluntary guidelines against overly thin models; and fashion officials in Madrid, who set a minimum body-mass index of 18 for their catwalk models.

Many tweens at the summit seemed to get the message. A 12-year-old said a stick-thin model made her "feel sick" because the model looked "un-normal".

If designers and magazines around the world took the lead, they could make *Brigitte*'s announcement that "a new epoch has begun" their own. Even if fatheads like Lagerfeld aren't willing to accept it.

USA today, October 14, 2009, Section 8 A

COMPREHENSION
Language Awareness

a. Read the newspaper article and collect (positive and negative emotive) words and phrases that support the statement made at the beginning that "too thin isn't 'in'".

pro 'thin'	against 'thin'
• Lagerfeld mocked … *Brigitte* • fat mummies …	• Lagerfeld … No longer. • …

ANALYSIS
Working with Visuals
→ FoS, Analysis of Visuals, p. 135

b. Compare the way the so-called "plus-size" model Crystal Renn poses on the cover of her autobiographic book to the pictures on page 37 of the Students' Book.
Describe the similarities and explain the intended effect.

10 No More Anorexic Models …

The New Pathway, p. 40

Frauenzeitschrift „Brigitte" zeigt keine magersüchtigen Models mehr

Es ist ein geradezu revolutionärer Schritt, den die Frauenzeitschrift „Brigitte" jetzt angekündigt hat: Als radikale Konsequenz aus dem anhaltenden Magenmodel-Trend wird „Brigitte" ab 2010 nicht mehr mit Profi-Models arbeiten. Statt magersüchtiger Schönheiten sollen künftig Mannequins der anderen Art die Seiten füllen. […]

Schon ab Anfang 2010 will „Brigitte" in sämtlichen Heften und auf allen Online-Seiten nicht mehr mit Profi-Models arbeiten. Chefredakteur Andreas Lebert kritisierte, dass jeder in der Branche wegen magersüchtiger Models dem anderen die Schuld in die Schuhe schiebe. Sein Magazin wolle einen eigenen Beitrag gegen diese Entwicklung leisten.

Damit reagiert die Frauenzeitschrift auf zwei große Trends: „Die Mode hat sich verändert – und die Frauen haben sich verändert", sagte Lebert. „Wir machen ein Blatt für Frauen, wie sie sind, und nicht wie andere sie gerne hätten," sagte der „Brigitte"-Chef. […]

Die Redaktion sei immer häufiger auch von Leserinnen darauf hingewiesen worden, dass sie „keine vorstehenden Knochen" mehr sehen wollten. Models würden heute 23 Prozent weniger wiegen als normale Frauen. Die gesamte Branche sei magersüchtig. Frauen wollen nach Leberts Ansicht keine Kleiderständer mehr sein; dies würden Umfragen und Leserbriefe bestätigen. […]

„Seit Jahren müssen wir die Mädchen mit Photoshop dicker machen, die Schenkel, das Dekolleté", sagte Lebert dem Nachrichtenmagazin „Spiegel". Das sei gestört und pervers: „Was hat das noch mit unserer echten Leserin zu tun? … Wir zeigen Mode an Insekten, und hinten im Heft sagen wir: Steh zu dir selbst, steh zu deinem Körper, die neuen Rezepte und so weiter."

www.welt.de/lifestyle/article4739357/Brigitte-zeigt-keine-magersuechtigen-Models-mehr.html [01.11.2009]

COMPREHENSION

Reading Comprehension
→ FoS, Reading Techniques, p. 59

a. Read the text and state its topic:

____

____

Language Awareness

b. Do a faithful translation of the highlighted verbs/collocations and adverbs/adverbials.

ACTIVITY

Mediation
→ FoS, Mediation, p. 123

c. Mediate the text into English – pay attention not to translate it literally, but focus on the most important information.

ANALYSIS

Working with Visuals
→ FoS, Analysis of Visuals, p. 134

d. The Austrian cartoonist Gerhard Haderer takes a critical look at the growing trend towards natural looking models.
Mediate the caption of the cartoon and relate it to the outward appearance and body language of the two 'models' presented in the cartoon.
Explain what the cartoonist wants to express.

Gerhard Haderer, *Ende der Dürreperiode: Die Models werden wieder molliger*

The New Pathway, p. 38, No. 1

11 Body Language and Outward Appearance

COMPREHENSION
Vocab Training

Look at the following adjectives and expressions describing outward appearance and body language and fill in the opposite word/expression.

outward appearance		body language	
tall		anxious	
overweight			hunched over
	formal		relaxed
	unattractive	posed	
stylish		lost in thought	
	fastened (shirt)	hectic	
	skintight (jeans)		self-confident
well-dressed			elegant
dark-haired		naïve	
	carelessly dressed	frowning	
neglected			friendly

The New Pathway, p. 37

12 One Man's Meat is Another Man's Poison …

COMPREHENSION
Synonyms
→ FoL, Improving Your Style, p. 130

The English proverb "One man's meat is another man's poison" shows how different people have different tastes – as is true in the field of beauty …
Use your dictionary and find as many synonyms as possible for the adjectives beautiful and ugly.

beautiful

____

ugly

____

13 Having a Go at the Human Body ...

The New Pathway, p. 37

The British painter Lucian Freud (*1922) says about painting, "I paint people not because of what they are like, not exactly in spite of what they are like, but how they happen to be." The American realist painter Edward Hopper (1882–1967) is considered to be one of the most famous contemporary painters who tried to convey the melancholy and loneliness of people.

Edward Hopper, *Girlie Show* (1941)

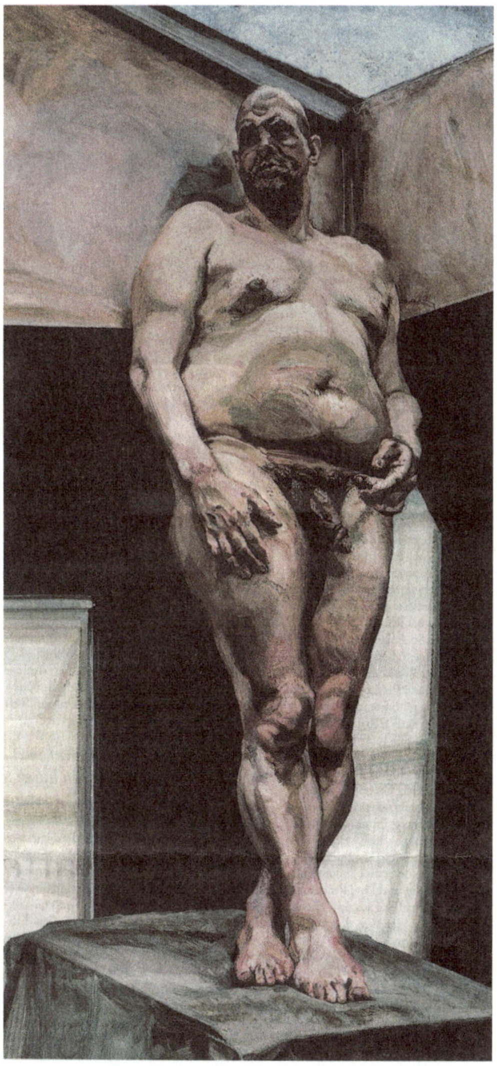

Lucian Freud, *Leigh under the Skylight* (1994)

Tips on vocab

an auction of paintings ■ sth. is up for auction ■ to sell/offer sth. at an auction ■ an Internet auction site ■ to auction sth. off ■ to bid on sth. ■ to outbid sb. ■ going once, going twice, sold to ... ■ to specialize in sth. ■ nude (painting) ■ unreserved provocative ■ disgusting ■ postmodern ■ realistic ■ oil on canvas painting

ACTIVITIES

Imagine you are working at the famous *Christie's* auction house in London. These two famous nude paintings by acclaimed painters are put up for auction and you have to describe and praise their quality and value to the bidders.

Working with Visuals
→ FoS, Analysis Visuals, p. 135

a. Do research on these artists and their respective backgrounds.

b. Describe the most important details and characteristics of the paintings.

c. Prepare a presentation in which you – as the auctioneer – inform the potential buyers.

Giving a Presentation
→ FoS, Presentation, p. 197

d. Act out the auction of the paintings in class.

e. Sometimes famous works of art are sold in Internet auctions. Design a website that promotes these two paintings.

The New Pathway, p. 40

14 Two Poems – One Size?!

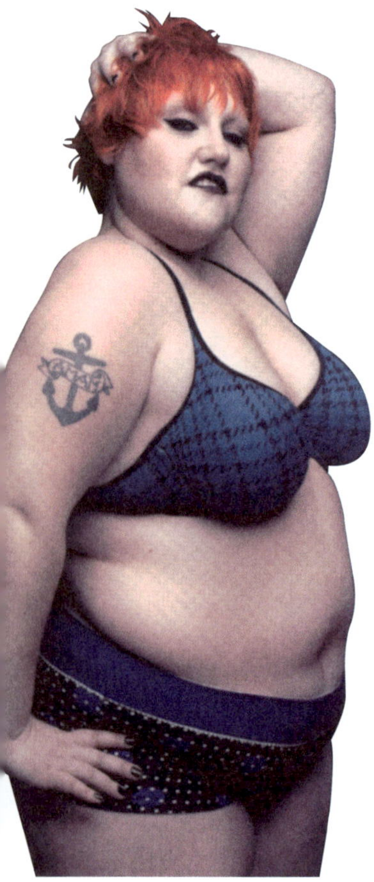

Beth Ditto, lead singer of the indie rock band *The Gossip*

Maya Angelou

Phenomenal Woman

Pretty women wonder where my secret lies.
I'm not cute or built to suit a fashion
model's size
But when I start to tell them,
They think I'm telling lies.
I say,
It's in the reach of my arms
The span[1] of my hips,
The stride[2] of my step,
The curl of my lips.
I'm a woman
Phenomenally[3].
Phenomenal woman,
That's me.

I walk into a room
Just as cool as you please,
And to a man,
The fellows stand or
Fall down on their knees.
Then they swarm around me,
A hive of honey bees[4].
I say,
It's the fire in my eyes,
And the flash of my teeth,
The swing in my waist,
And the joy in my feet.
I'm a woman
Phenomenally.
Phenomenal woman,
That's me.

Men themselves have wondered
What they see in me.
They try so much
But they can't touch
My inner mystery.
When I try to show them
They say they still can't see.
I say,
It's in the arch of my back[5],
The sun of my smile,
The ride of my breasts[6],
The grace of my style.
I'm a woman
Phenomenally.
Phenomenal woman,
That's me.

Now you understand
Just why my head's not bowed.
I don't shout or jump about
Or have to talk real loud.
When you see me passing
It ought to make you proud.
I say,
It's in the click of my heels,
The bend of my hair[7],
The palm of my hand[8],
The need of my care,
'Cause I'm a woman
Phenomenally.
Phenomenal woman,
That's me.

Lucille Clifton

Homage to My Hips

these hips are big hips.
they need space to
move around in.
they don't fit into little
petty places. these hips
are free hips.
they don't like to be held back.
these hips have never been enslaved,
they go where they want to go
they do what they want to do.
these hips are mighty hips.
these hips are magic hips.
i have known them
to put a spell[9] on a man and
spin him like a top[10].

[1] **span** here: the width of sth. from one side to the other – [2] **stride** your way of walking or running (e.g. in long steps) – [3] **phenomenal** [fə'nɒmɪnl] extraordinary – [4] **hive of bees** *Bienenkorb* – [5] **arch of sb.'s back** [ɑːtʃ] the curve that the back forms – [6] **ride** here: movement – [7] **bend** curve, turn – [8] **palm of sb.'s hand** the inner surface of the hand – [9] **to put a spell on sb.** *jdn. verzaubern* – [10] **to spin sb./sth.** to make sb. turn round and round quickly

a. Detect the imagery employed in these two poems and explain its function and effect on the reader.

ANALYSIS
Stylistic Devices
→ FoS, Analysis of Poetry, p. 155

poetic imagery		
stylistic device	**figurative meaning**	**effect**
metaphor • *they swarm around me …*		
personification • *they go where they want …*		
simile • *spin him like a top*		

b. Explain the meaning of the chorus of the first poem in your own words.
What does it reveal about the speaker's "secret" (l. 1)?

c. Choose one of the two given poems and write a structured analysis.

d. Compare the message of these two poems to the cartoon by Gerhard Haderer on p. 19 – in what way do the views differ?

e. Put yourself in the position of the "wondering men or women" watching this "phenomenal woman" and write an interior monologue of your thoughts and reflections.

ACTIVITIES
Creative Writing
→ FoS, Writing, p. 129

f. Gossip singer Beth Ditto has modelled for famous fashion labels. She has even promoted the underwear of famous fashion designers, wearing it onstage at concerts.
What do you consider to be the reasons for her popularity?
Discuss in class.

→ FoL, Holding a Conversation and Participating in a Discussion, p. 105

The New Pathway, p. 42

15 Disfigured – Learning to Accept Your Body

3, 4, 5

COMPREHENSION
Vocab Training

The last scene of the film shows Lydia founding her own self-help group – her aim is to make the participants accept and love their bodies.

a. Fill in the gaps in the text below with the following words. Some words/phrases can be used several times.

bodies	body parts	overweight	love	underweight
feelings	beauty	strange	acceptable	hate
fix them up	beautiful	us	pathetic	miraculous
accept	try			

“We are here to talk about our __________ **(1)**.

______________ **(2)** or ______________ **(3)** or changing weight – or maybe not having anything to do with ______________ **(4)** at all ...

Maybe we start with making a list of all our ______________ **(5)** ______________ **(6)**, just to get our ______________ **(7)** out.

But more importantly, I think that we just need to find a way to let our ______________ **(8)** in – because these bodies, they're __________ **(9)**.

And I don't understand how we can live in them all day, every day and still find them so ______________ **(10)**.

How can we ______________ **(11)** them?

They're ______________ **(12)**, and ______________ **(13)**, and ______________ **(14)**, and ______________ **(15)**.

And everything that we have in life we get through them.

I don't know, maybe we can help each other ______________ **(16)** a little. Sooner or later we just have to find a way to __________ **(17)** them for what they are.

To be able to __________ **(18)** what that looks like for each one of us.

I don't think that's going to happen any time soon – but we have to ______________**(19)**, we just have to ______________ **(20)**.

And I can't do that by myself ... ”

b. “ ... everything that we have in life we get through them [our bodies].”
State whether you agree or disagree with Lydia's statement.

16 Little Miss Sunshine: Body Language and Facial Expression

6, 7

The New Pathway, p. 43

Take a close look at the filmstills showing Olive and two other contestants at the beauty pageant and pay attention to the outward appearance of the girls.

ANALYSIS

Working with Film Stills
→ FoS, Analysis of a Film Scene, p. 20

a. Describe the body language and the facial expression of the people in the first two filmstills in as much detail as possible.

	contestant 1	contestant 2	Olive (3)
outward appearance	• *blonde, dolled-up hair*		
body language			
facial expression		• *artificial smile*	

b. Now describe Olive's body language and facial expression and compare her to the two other girls. What are the striking differences?

1

1:16:48

2

1:17:25

3 – Olive

1:28:47

c. Take a look at the audience (filmstill 4) and state what their outward appearance and body language reveals about them. Compare your findings to filmstill 5.

4

1:17:50

5

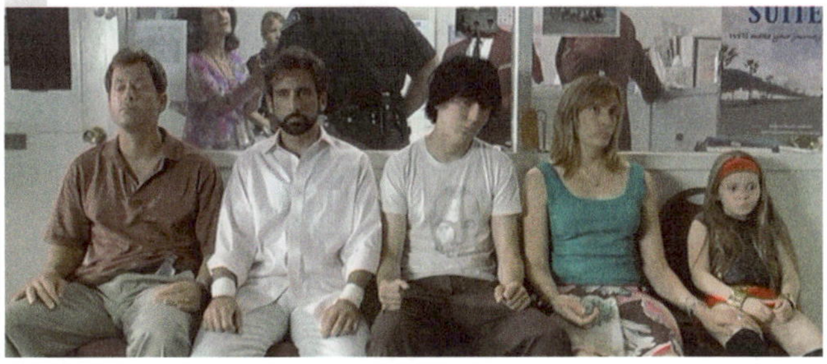

1:31:03

The New Pathway, p. 47

17 Children or Just Little Adults?

COMPREHENSION

Mediation
→ FoS, Mediation, p. 123

The following article was published in the German newspaper *Rheinische Post*, and focuses on the serious health damage that wearing high heels can cause.

a. Mediate this article, focusing on the most important aspects.

Suri Cruise (3) in Stöckelschuhen

LOS ANGELES Für helle Empörung in den USA sorgen derzeit die Lieblingsschuhe einer Dreijährigen: Suri Cruise, Tochter von Hollywood-Star Tom Cruise und seiner Frau Katie Holmes, trägt neuerdings auf vielen Paparazzi-Schnappschüssen goldene Schuhe – mit drei Zentimeter hohen Absätzen. So oft wurde die Kleine mittlerweile darin abgelichtet, dass Mutter Katie Holmes nun öffentlich stark in die Kritik geraten ist und zu den Vorwürfen von Ärzten Stellung beziehen musste.

Denn das häufige Tragen von Absatzschuhen kann laut Orthopäden bleibende Haltungsschäden bei einem Kind hinterlassen. „Die Knochen in ihren Füßen sind noch nicht voll ausgebildet", sagt Orthopäde Rüdiger Dohmann aus Düsseldorf. Kinder brauchten deshalb weite Schuhe mit einer verstärkten Fersenkappe, damit sich die Längs- und Querwölbung des Fußes richtig ausbilden könne. „Hochhackige Schuhe für ein Kind sind Schwachsinn."

Suri Cruise drohen laut Ärzten durch die Absätze Haltungsschäden.

Da sich viele amerikanische Orthopäden ähnlich entsetzt geäußert haben, hat sich Katie Holmes jetzt zu einem Statement genötigt gesehen: „Wie jedes kleine Mädchen liebt Suri meine hohen Absätze", erzählte Holmes laut „Usmagazine.com" in einem TV-Interview. Außerdem seien die Stöckelschuhe nur Tanzschuhe mit Absatz, die speziell für Kinder geeignet seien und die Füße somit nicht schädigen würden. „Ich fand die Schuhe für sie und Suri liebt sie", sagte Katie Holmes laut „Access Hollywood".

Für Dohmann sind die Rechtfertigungen der Mutter keine Entschuldigung. „Absätze verhindern ein richtiges Abrollverhalten des Fußes", sagt er. „Bei Kindern kann das zu Knick-, Senk- und Spreizfüßen führen, aber auch Schäden an der Wirbelsäule verursachen." Auch wenn die kleine Suri die Schuhe unbedingt tragen möchte, läge die Schuld eindeutig bei der Mutter, schließlich könne die Dreijährige noch nicht die Tragweite ihres Tuns erfassen. „Zu Absatzschuhen müssen die Eltern in jedem Fall Nein sagen."

In den USA hat der Vorfall vor allem deshalb an Brisanz gewonnen, da Suri Cruise als wohl süßester Promi-Spross Amerikas gilt und eines der meistfotografierten Kinder ist. Seit ihrer Geburt setzt das Mädchen Modetrends, stets kleidet Katie Holmes sie in Designermode. Bei Amerikas Müttern gilt Suris Stil als Vorbild, und was die kleine Cruise auf Paparazzi-Fotos trägt, ist oft binnen weniger Tage ausverkauft. Nun keimt die Sorge auf, dass die hochhackigen Kinderschuhe sich durchsetzen könnten. Für Dohmann wäre das eine gefährliche Entwicklung: „Kinder sind keine kleinen Erwachsenen", sagt er. „Sie brauchen Kleidung, die ihre körperliche Entwicklung fördert."

Tina Stockhausen, in: Rheinische Post, December 8, 2009, p. A 8

ACTIVITY

Language Awareness
→ FoL, Improving Your Style, p. 130

b. Find corresponding synonyms or paraphrases for these words:

adjective, verb, noun	synonym(s)	paraphrase
favourite (adj.)		
to damage (v.)		
to be shocked (v.)		
to love (v.)		
to realize (v.)		
spoilt (adj.)		
effect (n.)		
happy (adj.)		

c. Is wearing high heels or dressing up just child's play or can it seriously harm girls/boys? Against the background of the film *Little Miss Sunshine* and your findings about *JonBenét*, comment on the newspaper article and state your opinion.

ANALYSIS
Writing Practice
→ FoS, Writing a Comment, p. 33

18 Caught Between Shots and Shooting? – Violence and Drugs

The New Pathway, p. 50

Since 2008 the so-called "mosquito", a "teen repellent", has been a controversial topic in several European countries.

a. Read the following text and think about what grammatical tense to use in which context. Cross out the incorrect alternative.

GRAMMAR
Tenses
→ Grammar Kit, p. 211

Arjen Schreuder
Dutch Debate Use of 'Teen Repellent'

The mosquito, or "teen repellent," is intended to discourage groups of kids from loitering in the streets, making a nuisance of themselves or engaging in anti-social behavior. In the Dutch city of Rotterdam, its use has sparked a debate about the constitutionality of the controversial device.

"It sucks! It **gives/has given (1)** me a headache," 10-year-old Mohammed says, describing the "mosquito," a device that **emits/emitted (2)** an annoying sound with a frequency that can generally be heard only by people under the age of 25. His friends Ercan, Anass and Nordin **agree/have agreed (3)**. "It's like when **you've been listening/listened (4)** to loud music for a long time and then you stop," he says. "This buzzing sound."
The kids all **live/lived (5)** in Oud Charlois, a neighborhood in the Dutch city of Rotterdam where mosquitoes first **appeared/has appeared (6)** a year ago. We **take/took (7)** a walk from the Wolphaertsbocht to an interior court off Clemens Street. Within this small perimeter there **are/were (8)** no less than six mosquitoes: they're installed above snack bar Marlena, the clothing shop Hans, a bakery and a supermarket as well as in the courtyard itself. [...]
At Marlena's snack bar, **they've noticed/they had noticed (9)** that since last winter more and more kids **prefer/preferred (10)** to hang out inside the premises. But is it because of the mosquitoes buzzing outside? "I don't know," Marlena says. "All I know is they can be very annoying. They throw food around."
For their part, the local authorities in Oud Charlois **are/have been (11)** extremely pleased with the mosquitoes. "We **were/are (12)** getting complaints about intimidation and vandalism," says neighborhood council president Dick Lockhorst. "The nuisance **has diminished/had diminished (13)** by 70–80 percent. That means less work for the police."
Donald van der Laan, the general manager of the Rhine Consulting Group, a company that **imports/imported (14)** the mosquitoes for sale in the Netherlands, says he **has installed/had installed (15)** some 500 devices in 120 municipalities and the incidents of nuisance **have diminished/had diminished (16)** in nearly every location. He knows the Wolpaertsbocht area in Rotterdam. "It used not to be the kind of place I **will/would (17)** go after dark,", he says. "But it **improved/has improved (18)** a lot."
Still, the use of the mosquito **is/has been (19)** controversial – not only in the Netherlands, but also in Britain and other countries in Europe where it **was/has been deployed (20)**. An often-heard criticism is that the device affects everyone within a 20-meter (66-foot) radius, including people who are not creating a nuisance, such as sisters Saloua and Keltoum Azerkane and their friend Marwa Massali. "Whenever we pass by here, we get a headache," one says as the others express their agreement. [...]
Social workers in Charlois **are/have been (21)** extremely critical of the device. Jan Schellekens says, "It **has made/makes (22)** the kids irritable and aggressive. It makes them want to tear the device off the wall." Schellekens **has felt/feels (23)** the mosquito is the wrong tool. "All it **did/does (24)** is move the problem," she says. "Young offenders are forced even more underground so that they are even harder to reach. And there **was/is (25)** so little for the kids to do anyway. They **don't have/haven't had (26)** a place to go except the street. And now they **are being chased/are chased (27)** off the street."
The kids agree. "Where are we supposed to hang out?" asks one. "People say we are a menace. But we **don't do/haven't done (28)** anything. It's a free country, isn't it?" [...]

www.spiegel.de/international/europe/0,1518,621025,00.html [14.02.2010]

Pop-art print *Spray* by Roy Lichtenstein (1962)

ANALYSIS
Reading for Detail
→ FoS, Reading Techniques, p. 59

b. Point out reasons mentioned in the text for installing the "mosquito" and examine whether they can stand up to close examination.

c. The article implies that teenagers don't know what to do with themselves. Relate this impression to your findings concerning the bar charts on how ninth-graders spend their free time on pp. 52 f. in your Students' Book.

ACTIVITY
Language Awareness

d. Some words can be interpreted very differently depending on the individual perspective. Look up the meaning of the following words in your dictionary:

nuisance ______________________________ (1)

menace ______________________________ (2)

anti-social ______________________________ (3)

Explain how these definitions can be viewed differently.

The New Pathway, p. 56

19 Adults Only, Please – Child-Free Zone in Berlin Café Raises Eyebrows

Sometimes children can be really annoying. The following article describes a newly designed "child-free zone" in a Berlin neighbourhood café.

First it was smokers, now it is children. A Berlin café has excited debate by establishing a no-child section. For a nation with a low birthrate that is trying to encourage its citizens to have more babies, such an anti-child policy is cause for concern.

In the middle of one of the most child-friendly neighbourhoods in Berlin, one café is bucking the trend. In what appears to be a first for the German capital, the Café Niesen in Prenzlauer Berg has established a child-free zone on its own premises.
The café, which Christine Wick has run since 2005, is located in a cul-de-sac near a park and is opposite a petting zoo, which makes it the perfect place for parents to grab a drink or snack together with their offspring. But as Wick told the Berlin tabloid *B. Z.*: "My regulars were not finding it peaceful."
"Recently there were more and more parents with children, which is why we rented a premises to serve as a special, separate area for adults only," Wick, who has a 9-year-old son herself, told the mass circulation *Bild*.

Family-Friendly

Some reviews of Café Niesen describe the place as "family-friendly" – no traffic in the street, plenty of room for kids to play in and offering child-size snacks. Others, though, have noted the number of strollers parked outside and the screaming within. "It is best in the mornings. Or in the evenings – when all the little screamers of Prenzlauer Berg are safely tucked into bed," wrote Kristen Reinhardt in the daily *Die Tageszeitung* in 2008.

The café's new quiet room is marked with a sign reading "Only for Adults without Children." There is even a separate entrance so that adult patrons do not need to navigate a traffic jam of strollers to get inside.
Wick told *B. Z.* that only a few of her customers have complained about the separate area. But, outside the confines of her café, concern is growing. For years now, Germany has been troubled by its low birth rate, with the government in Berlin doing its best to encourage its citizens to have more babies. As such, any kind of anti-child sentiment is unwelcome – particularly in a neighbourhood like Prenzlauer Berg, with its dense population of toddlers.
For Social Democrat Stefanie Winde, who sits in the Berlin state parliament, the new child-free zone is "not acceptable." "We are a society that is having fewer children," the politician, who was recently told off for breastfeeding her daughter while sitting in the first row during a parliamentary session, told *Bild* "We need to be more tolerant." *cis*

www.spiegel.de/international/germany/0,1518.681951,00.html [06.03.2010]

a. Collect the arguments given in the text that support the idea of "adults only" and contrast them with arguments that hold to a "family-friendly" perspective.

COMPREHENSION
Reading Comprehension

pro adults only	pro family-friendly
• *not peaceful* • ...	• *social meeting place* • ...

b. Add further perspectives and discuss the pros and cons of the issue in class.
Here are some further ideas for discussion:
- an adult-free zone in certain restaurants/shops
- a zone for seniors only
- a zone for girls/boys only
- ...

ACTIVITY
Discussing Controversial Topics
→ FoL, Participating in a Discussion, p. 105

20 Teenage Boys: Nicer And Happier than People Think

The New Pathway, p. 51

GRAMMAR
Prepositions

a. Fill in the appropriate prepositions in the gaps.

Teenage boys in Britain are often seen as the bad guys _______ **(1)** society: they drink too much, behave badly and are lazy _____ **(2)** school. But a new survey[1] _____ **(3)** the Guardian newspaper paints a different picture. The survey of 1,000 teenage boys shows that most ________ **(4)** them are ambitious, happy _____ **(5)** home and think they will have a good career.

The survey found that 88 % of the boys interviewed thought that they had good career prospects, and 88 % saw themselves as ambitious. Most of the boys were happy ______ **(6)** their family lives (87 %), _____ **(7)** their social lives (87 %) and happy _____ **(8)** school or work (81 %).

They probably spend a bit too much time ______ **(9)** their computers, however: 57 % spend an average ______ **(10)** at least an hour a day ______ **(11)** social networking sites, with 21 % spending at least three hours a day _____ **(12)** sites like Bebo and MySpace. A third spent at least an hour playing online games, and 21 % watched YouTube ______ **(13)** an hour or more. Cyber bullying[2] was experienced by 21 % _____ **(14)** the boys.

Young males _______ **(15)** Britain get a bad press. A recent survey _______ **(16)** the British media showed that more than 60 % ________ **(17)** stories about teenage boys concerned crime. The most common word used to describe teenage boys _____ **(18)** the media was "yobs[3]".

Read On, December 2009, p. 6

[1] **survey** *Umfrage* – [2]**cyber bullying** bullying on the Internet – [3]**yob** (*fml.*) *Rüpel, Rowdy*

b. Collect the statistical data given in the newspaper article and turn it into a chart. Decide whether to use bar or pie charts. Compare and discuss your charts in class.

ANALYSIS
Working with Statistics
→ FoS, Analysis of Tables/Graphs/Charts, p. 163

c. Compare your findings to the bar charts on pp. 52 f. in your Students' Book and explain how the data (don't) match.

The New Pathway, p. 52

21 Teenagers Today – Like Father Like Son?

ANALYSIS

Working with Visuals
→ FoS, Analysis of Visuals, p. 134

a. "The apple never falls far from the tree" – as the proverb goes ...
Describe cartoons No. 1 and No. 2 and explain their meaning.

1

Now don't complain Mum:
You started it by giving me my first nose-ring ...

2

"I expect you all to be independent, innovative, critical thinkers who will do exactly as I say!"

b. Compare cartoons No. 1 and No. 3 and say in what way their messages differ.
Make use of connectives to improve your style.
Here are some examples:

Tips on vocab

compared to ■ similarly ■ but while the first ... ■ both ■ although ■ in contrast ■ on the contrary ■ that explains why ■ referring to ■ taking everything into account ■ therefore

c. The abbreviation "WWF" in cartoon 3 means "World Wrestling Foundation". Against this background, explain the meaning of the caption.

3

d. Describe cartoon No. 3 and pay attention to details:
- the family picture in the background
- the body language of the parents
- the outward appearance of the son (tattoo, facial expression, table manners, etc.)

e. Summing up the implied message of cartoon 3 and "The Miracles of Childhood" (Students' Book, p. 66), one could assume that teenagers are "mutant monsters". What do you think about dealing with young people in this way? Formulate your opinion in about 150 words. Share your views in class.

22 Unhappy, Unloved and Out of Control

The New Pathway, p. 56

ANALYSIS

Analysing Statistics
→ FoS, Analysis of Tables/Graphs/Charts, p. 163

a. First, look at these bar charts and write short answers to the following questions:

1. How did the numbers of students bullied at school develop until 2005?
2. What peaks concerning year and grades do the bars show?
   When and in which grades can the highest percentage of bullied students be found?
3. How much – percentage wise – does bullying differ between 6th and 12th grade?
4. Which kinds of schools had the most problems with school bullying? Make a ranking.
5. What were the most frequent reasons for discipline problems in the different schools?

School bullying (in %)

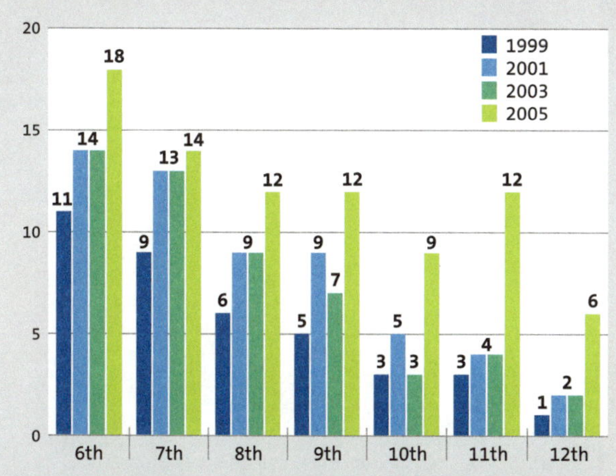

The percentage of students bullied at least once a week seems to have increased since 1999, although it is not clear whether the increase reflects more incidents of bullying at school or greater awareness of bullying as a problem.

Data: U.S. Department of Education, National Center for Education Statistics

Rates of bullying and other school discipline problems (in %)

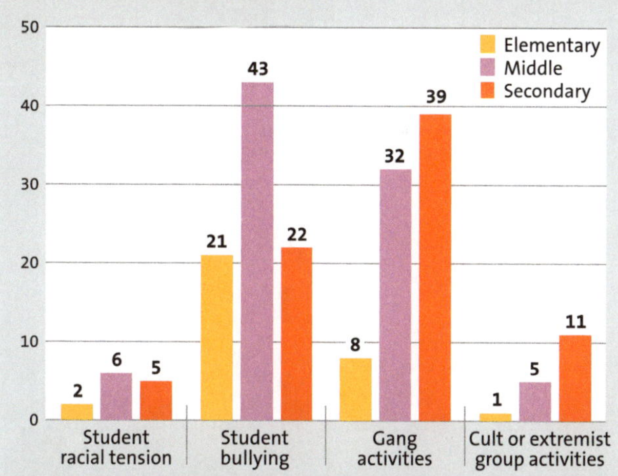

Student bullying is one of the most frequently reported discipline problems at school: 21 % of elementary schools, 43 % of middle schools, and 22 % of high schools reported problems with bullying in 2005–2006.

Data: U.S. Department of Education, National Center for Education Statistics

b. Now, write a description of each bar chart using your notes from above.

c. Collect the statistical data about European teenagers' drinking habits and involvement in violence on Students' Book pp. 56 ff. and turn them into a bar chart like the ones on this page.
Where do you find striking differences and similarities?

The New Pathway, p. 56

23 Once Upon a Time ... May Day ...

Many young people use the night before May Day as an opportunity to party – on the other hand, on May Day itself there are also violent demonstrations and riots.

ANALYSIS

Working with Visuals
→ FoS, Analysis of Visuals, p. 134

a. Describe the cartoon painted by Austrian cartoonist Gerhard Haderer and explain its message. Were things really so different in the old days?

Gerhard Haderer, *Tanz in den Mai*

Tips on vocab

Dance into May ■ bonfires ■ wrapping maypoles ■ to ask sb. for a dance ■ (open-air) dance floor ■ to go dancing ■ to court sb. ■ to bow to sb. ■ to riot/rioter/violent riots ■ police forces ■ to go on a rampage ■ hooligans ■ offensive/provocative slogans ■ violent fights ■ to set sth. on fire ■ to go to the barricades ■ to take action (in order to stop the fights)

24 Taking Different Views on Students Today ...

The New Pathway, p. 67

GRAMMAR
Indirect Speech
→ Grammar Kit, p. 215

a. Read the excerpts from different articles taken from British newspapers and turn all the sentences you can find from direct speech into indirect speech.

Students Living "Luxury Lifestyles"

Students are graduating with record debts because of their increasingly "luxurious lifestyles," according to a leading academic.

They are leaving university owing more than £20,000 each after spending huge sums on Marks & Spencer food, ipods and flat-screen TVs, it was claimed.
Kevin Sharpe, professor of Renaissance studies at Queen Mary, University of London, said typical student flats were now more likely trendy apartments seen in Friends, the Manhattan-based sitcom, than grimy bed-sits from The Young Ones.
[...] "In the town where I live at weekends, students pour not Aldi but Waitrose, with bottles of wine and champagne as well as bottled water, expensive foods and snacks," he said. "Taxi drivers lament the vacations, when their trade is depressed and whole parts of the city lose their bar and restaurant customers (I can hardly remember going out for dinner as a student). Student homes are often equipped with large LCD TVs, Sky boxes and, as burglars have been quick to spot, several high-end laptops per dwelling, offering richer pickings than normal domestic residences."
Research suggests that the average student already leaves with debts of up to £23,000, although some analysts claim the figure could be as high as £40,000. [...]
He added: "While for many that is doubtless financed by the bank of mum and dad, for those less well off but understandably anxious to keep up with their peers, the inevitable consequence is debt – and substantial debt at that."

Graeme Paton, www.telegraph.co.uk/education/educationnews/6274630 [11.03.2010]

Student Debt "Will Soar to £23,500"

The cost of higher education is set to rise by more than 10 per cent in coming years, prompting warnings that many students will be "priced out" of university.
[...] The National Union of Students warned that many teenagers gaining university places could be condemned to a "lifetime of debt."
Wes Streeting, NUS president, said: "With this year's new university students set to graduate with over £23,500 of debt, and graduate employment opportunities at an all-time low, we find it astonishing that universities continue to demand ever higher fees."
Sally Grunt, general secretary of the University and College Union, which represents academics, said: "It is criminal that generations of students will be saddled with thousands of pounds of debt. For all the talk of widening participation the sad reality is that students and their families are facing ever higher financial barriers to going to university." [...]
David Lammy, the Higher Education Minister, said: "Getting a degree remains a strong investment for a future career with graduates earning on average considerably more over a lifetime than people without a degree level qualification."

Graeme Paton, in: www.telegraph.co uk/education/educationnews/6042841 [11.03.2010]

Spiralling Debts and Poor Job Prospects Drive Sons – But Not Daughters – Home to Mum

Student debt, unaffordable house prices and rising unemployment is helping create a generation of mummy's boys. Unable to buy their own home, saddled with student debt and struggling to find work, grown-up sons are now twice as likely as their sisters to still be living at home with their parents, official statistics say. [...] Often those who stay at home are "boomerang children" who left home to go to university but then returned to the nest in early or mid-adulthood. [...] Roderick Orner, a consultant and clinical psychologist and visiting professor at Lincoln University, said: "There is a suspicion that many young people grow up these days being protected, shielded, almost spoiled by their parents. The critical experience of having to go and fend for yourself does not really arise as it used to do. Then they find themselves lacking in skills and it becomes difficult for them to do many things socially and financially and to form lasting relationships outside the family."

Independent Newspapers (UK) Ltd., in: World and Press, March 2, 2010, p. 6

COMPREHENSION

Reading for Detail
→ FoS, Reading Techniques, p. 59

b. Detect the information given in the articles about the reasons for student debts and depict their cause-effect relationship.

student lifestyles/cause for debts	effect(s)
• sitcom 'Friends' → trendy apartments • Marks & Spencer food • large LCD TVs • ...	→ spiralling debts → burglaries

The New Pathway, p. 55

25 Focus on Facts: The Media

COMPREHENSION

Reorganizing Information
→ FoF, The Media, p. 55

Read the *Focus on Facts* page in your Students' Book and fill in the information about the advantages and disadvantages of different kinds of media.

	advantages	disadvantages
print media		
electronic media		
personal media		

26 Owen Meany – Hester the Molester

The New Pathway, p. 61

A Word from the Author …

In developing his characters, Irving subjects them to extreme situations – "sexual situations or violent ones, whatever" – to bring out the "best and the worst aspects of ourselves … the things we admire or despise about people":

Basically I always try to place my characters under the most and least favorable circumstances to see how they will react, to test them. In Garp *this strategy was very self-conscious: I wanted to create characters whom I greatly admired and then bless them with incredibly good fortune in the first half of the novel … But in the second half of the novel, I visit all the worst kinds of extreme things on these people to see how they would deal with extremes of adversity, just as earlier they had to cope with success.*

This emotional extremes technique is most effective in Irving's bildungsroman motifs as children like T.S. Garp, the Berrys, Homer Wells, Johnny Wheelwright, and Owen Meany learn and mature from their experiences with life's extremes. […] Moreover, in refuting critics who fault him for the bizarre forces plaguing his fictional families, Irving retorts:

John Irving (*1942)

But let's take a simple family of four. Those two children will have, say, two children, making eight people. Is it claiming too much that out of the eight, someone is going to hit the wall? In a car crash, a plane crash, a wipeout, a premature tragedy, of course, it will happen! Someone is going off the deep end. They may not jump out a window, they make take drugs until they are useless, but certainly one of those eight isn't going to make it.

To complement the plot twists that carry his characters from fortune to misfortune, Irving juxtaposes the tragic with the comic. The tragic-comic extremes also drive his characters to the edge and determine their worth or worthlessness. Regarding life, Irving declares:

When people are happy – when we're in love, when we have orgasms of one kind or another, when we're proud of our children or high on ourselves – it strikes me that we are happy indeed. And who can say the world isn't comic, especially at those times? But we have pain too. Quite simply, the pain wins.

Edward C. Reilly: Understanding John Irving, Columbia, S.C., University of South Carolina Press, 1991, pp. 6 ff.

ANALYSIS

Narrative Techniques
→ FoS, Analysis of a Non-Fictional Text, p. 96

a. Explain John Irving's idea of "the emotional extremes technique" in your own words. What do you consider to be the function of this technique and its effect on the reader?

b. Go through the text (Students' Book, pp. 61 f.) again and find examples of tragic, comic and/or extreme elements.

line(s)	tragic elements	comic elements	extremes
13 ff.			• she'll fuck our whole class and leave you …
16 ff.		• … how do you date your first cousin?	

The New Pathway, p. 71

27 The Impact of the Media on Communication

Aislinn Laing

Teenagers Only Use 800 Different Words a Day

BBC television character Vicky Pollard, representing teenage delinquents with fast-paced, inarticulate speech

A generation of teenagers who communicate via the Internet and by text messages are risking unemployment because their daily vocabulary consists of just 800 words, the Government's new children's communication tsar has warned.

Although, according to recent surveys, they know an average of 40,000 words, they tend to favour a "teenspeak" used in text messages, on social networking sites and in Internet chat rooms like MSN[1].

One poll, commissioned by Tesco[2], revealed that while children had the vocabulary to be articulate, the top 20 words they used – including the Vicky Pollard lexicon of "yeah", "no" and "but" accounted for about a third of all the words they used.

According to Jean Gross, England's first Communication Champion for Children who started in the post this month, the lack of range will impact negatively on their chances of getting a job. Miss Gross is planning to launch a nationwide campaign next year to ensure children use their full language potential and are not impeded[3] in the classroom and later, the workplace, because they are inarticulate. [...]

"Teenagers are spending more time communicating through electronic media and text messaging, which is short and brief," she told *The Sunday Times*. "We need to help today's teenagers understand the difference between their "textspeak" and the formal language they need to succeed in life. 800 words will not get you a job." [...]

Both Marks & Spencer[4] boss Sir Stuart Rose and Tesco's Sir Terry Leahy have recently lamented the lack of school-leavers with the right skills for the workplace.

John Bald, a language teaching consultant and former Ofsted[5] schools inspector, said the poor use of language was a deliberate, anti-establishment act.

"There is undoubtedly a culture among teenagers of deliberately stripping away excess verbiage[6] in language," he said.

"When kids are in social situations, the instinct is to simplify. It's part of a wider anti-school culture that exists among some children which parents and schools need to address."

But David Chrystal, honorary professor of linguistics[7] at Bangor University in Wales, told *The Sunday Times* that experts simply do not understand the complexities of teen language and had judged it by their own standards.

"The real issue here is that people object to kids having a good vocabulary for hip-hop and not for politics," he said. "They have an articulate vocabulary for the kind of things they want to talk about. Few academics[8] get anywhere near measuring that vocabulary."

www.telegraph.co.uk/education/educationnews/6960745/Teenagers-only-use-800-different-words-a-day.html [23.04.2010]

[1] **MSN** The Microsoft Network, a collection of Internet sites and services provided by Microsoft – [2] **Tesco** Britain's largest merchandising retail chain – [3] **to impede** to make it difficult to move forward or make progress – [4] **Marks & Spencer** a major British retailer – [5] **Ofsted** The Office for Standards in Education, Children's Services and Skills, a government department responsible for the inspection of standards of schools in Britain – [6] **excess verbiage** speech or writing that has many unnecessary words – [7] **linguistics** the scientific study of languages – [8] **academic** a person who teaches and/or does research at a university

COMPREHENSION

Reading Comprehension

a. What, according to the author, are the risks of "teenspeak" and/or "textspeak"?

Language Awareness
→ FoL, The Language Register of English, p. 76

b. The article itself is written in formal or Standard English.
Find equivalents in everyday English for the words and expressions highlighted in the article.

Here is an example:
l. 5 communication tsar – an authority/expert on communication/language education

c. Decode and translate the text messages into Standard English.

B4YKI	2GTBT	XME	DYHAG	WUZ4dina
DNBL8	CF	10Q	I<3U	B4
AITR	BB4N	G2G	DYHAB	4eva
UOK	4COL			

ACTIVITY
Language Awareness

28 The Benefits of the Media in Everyday Life

The New Pathway, p. 71

a. Describe the cartoons and explain what topic in particular they are hinting at.

b. Explain the message of the cartoons and say whether they are convincing and effective.

ANALYSIS
Analysing Cartoons
→ FoS, Analysis of Visuals, p. 134

1

"JUST THINK OF IT AS IF YOU'RE READING A LONG TEXT-MESSAGE."

2

"Okay. Now, try to parallel park while talking on your cell phone and changing songs on your iPod."

3

c. Comment on the cartoons. Say whether you agree or disagree with their message.

ACTIVITY
Writing Practice
→ FoS, Writing a Comment, p. 33

The New Pathway, p. 72

29 The Funeral of a Superstar as a Media Moment

COMPREHENSION

Skimming a Text
→ FoS, Reading Techniques, p. 59

a. Skim the article about Michael Jackson's funeral in your Students' Book (pp. 72 f.) again and point out the most important information given in each paragraph.

lines	information
1–6	*relevance of the topic; worldwide interest in the news coverage; …*
7–14	
15–23	
24–30	
31–39	
40–42	
43–49	
50–60	
61–67	
68–79	

Summary Writing
→ FoS, Writing, p. 129

b. Now, after collecting the most relevant information, write a summary of the article in about 100–150 words.

Follow the structure: introductory sentence – main part, consisting of factual information only – a concluding sentence.

Do not write about unimportant details and avoid emotive words.

ACTIVITY

Creative Writing
→ FoS, Writing, p. 129

c. Although Michael Jackson was an international superstar people view(ed) him very differently. Whereas many fans absolutely adored him, some people have remained very critical of his way of life. It is the custom to find words of praise for a public figure after his death, and the obituaries generally stress the good qualities. Nevertheless they might hint "gently" at a person's shortcomings and trespasses.

Imagine you have to find appropriate "last words" from different perspectives, expressing either grief … relief … fear … anger … hope, etc.
Write an obituary about Michael Jackson.

The New Pathway, p. 74

30 An Interview with P!nk

GRAMMAR

Asking Questions

P!nk is known for writing and singing about personal experiences …

a. Read the song text (Students' Book, pp. 74 f.) again, and find out what clues are given here where she reveals something personal.

You want to know more about her – now you have to ask the right questions …

- Formulate questions for an interview – but avoid questions that can be answered with 'yes' or 'no' – ask open questions or questions after a short statement.
- Pay attention to the word order – and try to vary the beginning of the questions, e. g. by using different question words (who – where – when – what – why …).

Examples:

- *What actually made you write about and reveal such personal experiences as you did in the song "Family Portrait"?*
- *In what way did your revelations affect your family?*
- *If you could do things over, would you have revealed less about your life?*

31 Focus on Language: The Language Register of English

The New Pathway, p. 76

Mark Twain's popular novel *The Adventures of Tom Sawyer*, published in 1876, deals with the friendship of Tom Sawyer and his best friend, Huckleberry Finn.
Whereas Tom, together with his brother, lives with his caring Aunt Polly, Huck has to take care of himself. His father is a drunkard and Huck himself has never attended a school. In the course of the novel he is adopted by the wealthy Widow Douglas who tries to "civilize" and educate Huck – which is really hard on Huck. In the given extract Huck is complaining about his misery to his best friend Tom.

"Don't talk about it, Tom. I've tried it, and it don't work; it don't work, Tom. It ain't[1] for me; I ain't used to it. The widder's[2] good to me, and friendly; but I can't stand them ways. She makes me git up just at the same time every morning; she makes me wash, they comb me all to thunder[3]; she won't let me sleep in the woodshed; I got to wear them blamed clothes that just smothers[4] me, Tom; they don't seem to any air git through 'em, somehow; and they're so rotten nice that I can't set down, nor lay down, nor roll around anywhere's; I hain't[5] slid[6] on a celler door for – well, it spears to be years; I got to go to church and sweat and sweat – I hate them ornery[7] sermons! I can't catch a fly in there, I can't chaw. I got to wear shoes all Sunday. The widder eats by a bell; she goes to bed by a bell; she gits up by a bell – everything's so awful reg'lar a body can't stand it."

"Well, everybody does that way, Huck."

"Tom, it don't make no difference. I ain't everybody, and I can't *stand* it. It's awful to be tied up so."

Mark Twain: The Adventures of Tom Sawyer, New York, Airmont Books, 1962, pp. 218 f.

HUCKLEBERRY FINN

[1] **ain't** (*coll.*) am not/is not/are not – [2] **widder** widow – [3] **to comb sb. to thunder** here: to comb sb.'s hair excessively – [4] **to smother** (almost) kill sb. by covering him too much – [5] **hain't** (*coll.*) haven't – [6] **slide (slid, slid) on a cellar** here: to climb down into a cellar (to sleep there) – [7] **ornery** bad-tempered

a. Read the extract from the novel and mark the orthographically or grammatically incorrect words and phrases as well as the colloquialisms and slang expressions.

b. Rewrite the text, using Standard English, the correct spelling and the grammatically correct formulation.

c. Discuss whether Huck's complaints make sense to you.
Which "burdens of civilization" are necessary and/or useful and which behaviour or habit does not make any sense at all?
What advice would you give Huck?

GRAMMAR

Language Awareness
→ FoL, The Language Register of English, p. 76

Correcting Mistakes

ACTIVITY

Discussion
→ FoL, Participating in a Discussion, p. 105

The New Pathway, p. 77

32 Strictly a Family Matter ...?!

The cartoon focuses on very modern trends in families worldwide.

ACTIVITY
Working with Visuals
Mediation
→ FoS, Mediation, p. 123

a. Mediate the cartoon and explain what contemporary trends in education, child raising and family it is referring to.

Tips on vocab

the birth of Jesus ■ the stable of Bethlehem ■ the Gospel of Luke ■ the (Biblical) Nativity story ■ the Three Wise Men/the Magi [ˈmeɪdʒaɪ] ■ Christmas Eve ■ the holy Family ■ manger ■ stable ■ starry sky ■ to present a gift

The New Pathway, p. 78

33 Choosing to Be Childless

In the grid in your Students' Book on p. 78 a variety of "Why Nots" are offered explaining why many couples today choose to be childless.

ACTIVITY
Finding Counterarguments
→ FoS, Analysis of Tables/Graphs/Charts, p. 163

a. Put yourself in the opposite position, e. g. the position of a Minister of Family Affairs, and try to refute (*widerlegen, entkräften*) the arguments given.

against having children	pro having children
• concern about future	• children are the future – without them there will be no future at all ...
• no steady partner	
• enjoy current lifestyle ...	
• ...	

34 Focus on Vocab

The New Pathway, p. 79

COMPREHENSION
Vocab Training

a. Complete the table by using the thematic vocabulary pages of this unit in your Students' Book on pp. 79 ff. If necessary, check your dictionary.

noun	adjective	verb
adolescence		
	young	
		to criticize
grown-up		
		to date
	(to be) jealous of sb.	
puberty		
	tempting	
		to violate
attractiveness		
	educated	
graduation		

Collocations

b. Combine the words and phrases from the box and form **collocations** (= a combination of words). Some words can be used more than once.

Example:
- *to reach the age of majority*

role • youth control • to make • sex • test • majority • to do sth. • safer sex • experience • legal • group • addiction • to be tempted • abuse • drinking • physical • to take • violation • to be • eating • body • fat • ideal • domestic • to reach • secondary • pressure • binge • a particular weight • primary • model • culture • birth • love • to have • pregnancy • the age (of) • to aim • to practice • to gain • emancipation • peer • drug(s) • habit • violence • rule • disorder • weight • intake • quarrel • education

Nature & Environment: Go Green – Save the Earth?!

The New Pathway, p. 83

1 Discourse Analysis of (Political) Songs 7

How would you characterize and evaluate this song?

Circle the number of your choice: 1 = not at all; 6 = very much

warm/gentle	1 2 3 4 5 6
ecologically critical	1 2 3 4 5 6
coarse	1 2 3 4 5 6
lively	1 2 3 4 5 6
soft	1 2 3 4 5 6
boring	1 2 3 4 5 6
simple	1 2 3 4 5 6
aggressive	1 2 3 4 5 6
fun	1 2 3 4 5 6
shocking	1 2 3 4 5 6
appalling	1 2 3 4 5 6
accusatory	1 2 3 4 5 6
cynical	1 2 3 4 5 6
good vocals	1 2 3 4 5 6
repetitive	1 2 3 4 5 6
good beat	1 2 3 4 5 6
good instrumentation	1 2 3 4 5 6
good lyrics	1 2 3 4 5 6
socio-political	1 2 3 4 5 6
disorganized	1 2 3 4 5 6
too long	1 2 3 4 5 6
too slow	1 2 3 4 5 6
Registers of English:	
poetic	1 2 3 4 5 6
colloquial	1 2 3 4 5 6
archaic	1 2 3 4 5 6

slang/non-standard English	1 2 3 4 5 6
technical/scientific terms	1 2 3 4 5 6
makes me want to dance	1 2 3 4 5 6
inspiring	1 2 3 4 5 6
soothing	1 2 3 4 5 6
lyrics and music match	1 2 3 4 5 6
I want to hear it again	1 2 3 4 5 6
I would give it to a friend	1 2 3 4 5 6
I think the person singing is:	
sincere	1 2 3 4 5 6
in love	1 2 3 4 5 6
excited	1 2 3 4 5 6
convincing	1 2 3 4 5 6
angry	1 2 3 4 5 6
bored	1 2 3 4 5 6
boring	1 2 3 4 5 6
courageous	1 2 3 4 5 6
frightened	1 2 3 4 5 6
I would like to meet the singer:	1 2 3 4 5 6

Further comments:

____

____

____

What would you like to change about the song?

Adapted from: Barry Tomalin, Susan Stempleski: Cultural Awareness, Oxford, Oxford University Press, 1993, p. 25 and Tim Murphey: Music and Song, Oxford, Oxford University Press, pp. 84ff.

COMPREHENSION

Understanding Lyrics → FoS, Listening Comprehension, p. 117

a. Listen to the song *Go Green* again as well as to the introductory remarks spoken before. Then re-read the song text on p. 82 of your Students' Book. Use the grid for a first evaluation and characterization of the song and its instrumentation.

b. Summarize the song in 1–2 sentences. Try to answer the w-questions (who, what, where, when, why) in your introductory sentences.

ANALYSIS

Analysing Lyrics → FoS, Analysis of Poetry and Lyrics/Songs, p. 155

c. Now, analyse the song and the introductory remarks, using your previous notes and taking the song's lyrics as well as its musical elements into consideration.

2 Pronunciation and Phonetic Spelling

7

The New Pathway, p. 83

ACTIVITIES
Pronunciation Practice

Use the pronunciation and phonetic symbols given on p. 6 of the Workbook and spell these words taken from the song text *Go Green*.

vocabulary	pronunciation/phonetic spelling
governments	
worth	
corrupt	
maximization	
lead	
ozone layer	
fertile	
multinationals	
leak	
ecological	
profit	
earth	ɜːθ (BE) / ɜːrθ (US)
acid rain	
to pour	
premature	

3 Crime Scene Earth?!

The New Pathway, p. 83

ANALYSIS
Analysing Cartoons
→ FoS, Analysis of Visuals, p. 134

a. Examine the two cartoons and relate them to the song *Go Green*.
Write a short text of about 100–150 words in which you state to what extent they match the message of the song text.

The New Pathway, p. 87

4 Focus on Facts: Eco Fashion

COMPREHENSION
Memorizing Information
→ FoF, Eco Fashion, p. 87

a. Study the *Focus on Facts* page in your Students' Book on p. 87 carefully. Then explain these words and terms.

eco fashion terminology	your explanation
eco fashion	
fast fashion	
slow fashion	
manufacturing	
must-haves	
disposable couture	
trans-seasonal	
sustainable consumption	
environmental footprint	
ethical fashion	

ANALYSIS
Expressing an Opinion

b. Explain the title of the book cover *Green is the New Black* (Students' Book, p. 87).

c. Do you share the opinion that eco fashion is absolutely 'cool and hip'?

d. Explain in what way the cartoon addresses the topic.

"… so I decided to make us all fabulous new outfits from the Guardian environment supplement!"

5 How Much 'Stuff' Is Really Necessary?

The New Pathway, p. 88

Ann Cartwright
Budget

A Family Meeting

DAD: The actual reason I called this meeting is because of the family holiday we are taking this summer.

SOPHIE: To the villa in Spain!

GAVIN: Instead of last year's pokey hotel room in Spain.

TINA: With dripping taps. A deliberate decision to drive us mad. And they couldn't take the 'flea-ridden-dump' criticism. I mean, hello? Problem or what?

GAVIN: Could somebody pull her batteries out, please?

TINA: Could somebody stamp on Gavin, please?

DAD: If we are having this holiday in Spain, this very *expensive* holiday in Spain, then we are going to have to *budget*. [...]

MUM: (*entering*) [...] Good evening, family. How is my little brood?

DAD: I'm just telling them about how we've got to budget to be able to afford the villa in Spain.

MUM: True. Is that as far as we've got? I didn't miss anything else?

DAD: No. I am just about to tell them *how* we are going to budget.

SOPHIE: I don't like that emphasis on the word 'how'. Do you, Tina?

TINA: It sounds as if it is something we will not like.

MUM: You will *not* like it, Tina. You are quite right. We never do anything in this family that you children will like, you know that. (*To Dad*) Tell them, Beloved.

DAD: We're going to stop *buying* things!

MUM: Easy, isn't it? (*Gavin gives her tea.*) Is this for me? How sweet of you to do that without having your arm twisted up behind your back.

GAVIN: (*sitting back down*) I take it the stop-buying remark was aimed solely at us, right?

DAD: No, no, no. Your mum and I will be budgeting as well. It's just that it will affect you three more, as it is you three who bring the most pointlessly-expensive garbage into this house.

SOPHIE: I see. And I'll bet you've made a list, haven't you?

MUM: We certainly have. Now then, no more rubbish can come into this house. Not even a little bit. Fashion, my chicks, is dead.

DAD: When all the other young people are buying the latest media-hyped craze, you will not be.

MUM: You will be saving your pennies and putting them into your piggy-banks for the holiday, when you can then do splishy-splashy in the villa's private swimming pool. Won't that be so much nicer than a silly old pair of jeans that you don't want in the first place. Hm?

SOPHIE: May I say ...

DAD: The Chair recognizes Sophie.

SOPHIE: Thank you. May I say that I do not bring rubbish into this house. I am certainly not influenced by the media. I make my own choices. I only buy what I need.

DAD: (*controlling himself*) Sophie, pet, you are wearing a hat with a tiger's head and paws on the front of it.

SOPHIE: This is high fashion. Everyone's wearing them. Haven't you seen the ads on the telly? I'm not going to be left out.

GAVIN: Fashion victim. Controlled by the media. It's sad, really.

MUM: How much did you pay for it?

SOPHIE: Can't remember.

GAVIN: £10.99.

SOPHIE: That's a lie!

GAVIN: I was with you when you bought it.

SOPHIE: Oh, yes! That was the day you bought the new trainers. The top fashion ones with the sound effects in the soles. You know. The ones you don't wear anymore because all your mates were laughing at you. How much were they now, Gavin? Two quid? Three quid? Surely not more?

GAVIN: Can't remember.

TINA: Fifty quid! At least! Squandering money!

GAVIN: Ah, but they were essential. I couldn't go around barefoot, could I?

SOPHIE: You don't wear them at all! They're at the back of your wardrobe with the dust and the spiders.

GAVIN: Well, how was I to know that fashions would change that fast? And anyway, who begged for a micro-scooter then and never uses it now?

TINA: I ... don't remember ... doing that ... [...]

DAD: Then we have the main drains on resources. Firstly, games. Sophie and Gavin – beserk buyers and demanders of Game Boy stuff and CD Roms. They announce it – you buy it. Forever keeping up with your friends.

MUM: I'm fed up of seeing you squatting over the Game Boy thing. Every time I walk into the room, you're staring intently at your knees or waggling that handset around. Not only is it expensive – frankly, I think it's weird.

GAVIN: It's the modern entertainment!

SOPHIE: Everybody does it!

Ann Cartwright: Big Issues, Scripts and Sketches for Citizenship, Oxford, Heinemann Plays, 2002, pp. 2 ff.

COMPREHENSION

Reading Comprehension
→ FoS, Reading Techniques, p. 59

a. In the family meeting everybody wants to make a point. Read the scene again and select the arguments given for and against (not) buying certain things.

family member	arguments for/against	refutation (counterargument)
Mum	• *Fashion, my chicks, is dead.* • …	
Dad	• …	
Sophie	• *You don't wear them at all!* • …	• *Everybody does it!*
Tina	• …	
Gavin	• *It's the modern entertainment!*	

b. In a second step, skim the text again and detect how the family members try to refute each others' arguments and add them to the grid.

ANALYSIS

Text Analysis

c. Compare the arguments given and state whether they are convincing (or not).

GRAMMAR

Adverbs
→ Grammar Kit, p. 219

d. Choose adverbs from the grid below and add them to the statements of the family members. Be careful to put them in the right position.

Example: (l. 6 f.) *A deliberate decision to drive us absolutely mad.*

adverbs of manner	adverbs of frequency	adverbs of place	adverbs of time	adverbs of degree	sentence adverbs
well	never	here	yesterday	extremely	fortunately
beautifully	always	there	today	hardly	undoubtedly
happily	often	everywhere	tomorrow	very	luckily
quickly	sometimes	up	now	quite	probably
enthusiastic	usually	down	then	rather	generally
heavily	twice	inside	yet	completely	
cheaply	repeatedly	outside	already	considerably	
cheerfully	just	in England	at 8 o'clock	totally	
successfully	eventually		in the evening	constantly	
			on May 22, 1980	absolutely	
			all day		

ACTIVITY

Working with Statistics
→ FoS, Analysis of Graphs/ Tables/Charts, p. 163

e. First, mediate and describe the statistics in the "piggy bank", which covers the answers given by 6-13-year-olds.

Then, do a brief survey in your class/grade and say whether/to what extent the numbers change. If necessary, add further items (e.g. fashion).

WOFÜR SPAREN KINDER?

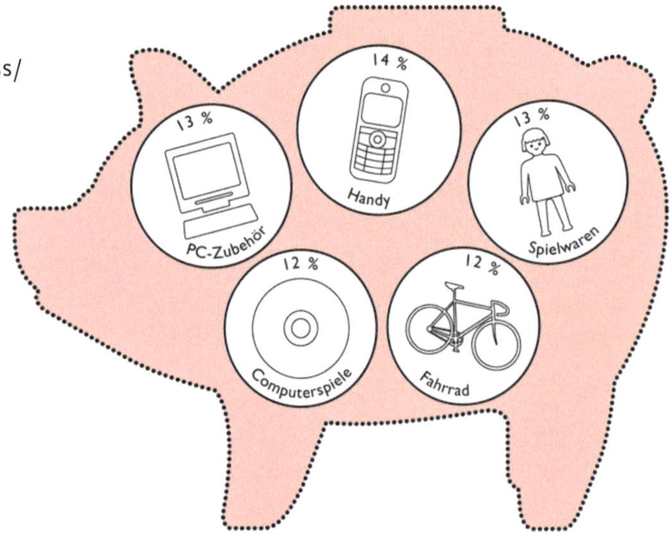

6 Waste Couture – The Environmental Impact of the Clothing Industry

The New Pathway, p. 88

1

Each step of the clothing production process potentially impacts the environment. For example, conventionally grown cotton, one of the most popular clothing fibers, is also one of the most water- and pesticide-dependent crops.
At the factory stage, effluent may contain a number of toxins. (Above: waste products from a garment factory in Dhaka, Bangladesh, spill into a stagnant pond.)

2

Textile workers form China commonly spray-dye jeans for deep color or stonewash them for a fashionable distressed look. The blue dust from the jeans is a heavy irritant to the lungs. The so-called wear-and-tear process is used for the production of approximately 10,000 pairs of jeans per day. Thousands of workers labor around the clock scrubbing, spraying, and tearing jeans in order to meet the production demand. China is one of the world's largest producers of jeans.

based on Environmental Health Perspectives, Volume 115, No. 9, Sep 2007, pp. A 450, A 452

COMPREHENSION

Describing Photographs
→ FoS, Analysis of Visuals, p. 134

a. Describe the photographs, paying attention to details. Employ adjectives in your description to capture and depict the appalling situation.

1 Tips on vocab

back yard ■ disgusting ■ ghastly sight ■ piles (of rotting textiles) ■ scattered garbage ■ sewage/effluents seeping into the ground ■ polluted water (pond) ■ muddy ■ greasy ■ filthy ■ smelly ■ toxic ■ unhealthy ■ cotton field ■ cotton reaper ■ fields stretching to infinity/to the horizon ■ blue skies

2 Tips on vocab

exhausted ■ to wear a mask over one's mouth ■ colour-stained ■ covered with dust ■ fashion house/jeans shop ■ rows of jeans on hangers ■ vintage look ■ destroyed look ■ bleached ■ sanded ■ stone-washed ■ torn up ■ used look ■ wear-and-tear look

ACTIVITY

Planning a Campaign
→ FoS, Writing, p. 129

b. Use your previous descriptions and results and plan a campaign.
Design posters and adverts to make people aware of the appalling social and environmental conditions. Try to find catchy phrases for your campaign.

The New Pathway, p. 88

7 Sustainable Style – Eco Fashion Show

Nachhaltig schön

Eco-Design heißt das Stichwort, unter dem sich dieses Jahr in Portland, Oregon internationale Models, Modemacher und Ökodesigner zum Schaulaufen treffen. Lufthansa unterstützt als einer der Hauptsponsoren die Fashion Week in der Stadt, die als grünste und nachhaltigste der Vereinigten Staaten gilt. Vom 7. bis 11. Oktober dreht sich auf der Messe alles um die umweltverträgliche Herstellung von Design und Mode. Da große Konzerne die Veranstaltung fördern, fallen für die Teilnehmer nur geringe Gebühren an. So erhalten auch herstellerunabhängige Designer die Chance, sich zu präsentieren. Die Messe selbst geht mit gutem Beispiel voran: Der Laufsteg ist aus recycelbaren Materialien gebaut, die Models benutzen ausschließlich umweltvertragliche Kosmetika und die Gäste werden in Hotels mit Öko-Siegel untergebracht. Informationen unter www.portlandfashionweek.net.

Lufthansa Magazin 09/2009, p. 22

ACTIVITIES

Mediation
Presenting a Fashion Show
→ FoS, Mediation, p. 123
→ FoS, Presentations, p. 197

a. Read the text about Portland Fashion Week and mediate it.
Use the information given in the text and present/introduce the models wearing eco-fashion. Employ positive emotive words and/or superlatives for your presentation.

Tips on vocab

gown ■ evening dress ■ robe ■ trend colour (nude) ■ frills (= *Rüschen*) ■ delicate fiber ■ transparent ■ excellent quality ■ swinging ■ ankle-length ■ knee-length ■ extravagant design ■ flared skirts ■ layers of cloth ■ high-end quality

8 Shop Till You Drop …

The New Pathway, p. 88

ACTIVITY
Language Awareness

a. Fill the respective words and phrases into the gaps.

shopping	consumer-based	forbidden	environment	destroying
energy	horror	dangerous	clever	toxins
things	better	new fashions	wasteful	hidden
manufacturers	plastic	teach	negative	resources
close	population	too much	poisonous	garbage
consumer				

A Short Animated Movie by Greenpeace Activist Annie Leonard Has Become a Big Hit in US Schools

When Annie Leonard and Free Range productions designed *The Story of Stuff* in 2007, they didn't know that they had just made a blockbuster movie. Today, it has been seen by more than 7 million people in 228 countries. Why? Because it's the world's most interesting film about ______________ **(1)**! *The Story of Stuff* is a very simple black-and-white animation that does exactly what it says on the cover: it tells us everything we need to know about the ______________ **(2)** we buy, but it's actually a ______________ **(3)** movie about shoppers like you and me ______________ **(4)** the planet.

According to Annie Leonard, most people don't even know about the ______________ **(5)** dangers of buying modern ______________ **(6)** goods. The problem is that we use far ______________ **(7)** stuff, and mass production is not only ______________ **(8)** but also quite ______________ **(9)**. Every American makes 4.5 pounds of ______________ **(10)** every day. For every pound of household junk, the ______________ **(11)** produce another 70 pounds.

The Story of Stuff also tells us that American factories produce at least 4 billion pounds of ______________ **(12)** every year. Poisons like dioxin are at least as ______________ **(13)** as radioactivity, but thousands of tons are still buried in the ground and blown into the air just because we need things like ______________ **(14)** water bottles.

Leonard's countrymen make up about 5 % of the world's ______________ **(15)** but they use up 30 % of the world's ______________ **(16)**. How do they manage to do this? Because only 1 % of the products bought in America are still in use after six months. Advertising and television create ______________ **(17)** every week, so people are made to want new things all the time. However, it would be very hard to change this, because the US is a ______________ **(18)** economy: if people stop shopping, factories will ______________ **(19)** and the money will stop flowing, resulting in a recession.

Many US schools have begun using Leonard's video clip to ______________ **(20)** their students more about saving the ______________ **(21)**. However, it has also been attacked by conservative

Americans because it's aggressive and not objective enough. The state of Montana has even ______________ (22) teachers to show it in schools, because a parent complained that there "was not one positive thing about capitalism in the whole thing." He is right: the movie is ______________ (23) and easy to understand but it's also quite ______________ (24). It tells us what's wrong with the economy but it does not teach us how to become ______________ (25) shoppers. However, Annie Leonard's new website does teach us about saving ______________ (26) and resources.

Check it out at: www.thestoryofstuff.com.

John Bilstein: The Story of Stuff gives American shoppers something to think; in: Read On, December 2009, p. 7

COMPREHENSION
Restructuring Information

b. Collect the facts that are given in the article about
- the hidden dangers of modern consumer goods,
- the production of garbage,
- the role of the USA as a consumer-based economy.

Mind Mapping

c. Arrange your previous findings in a mind map. You can start like this:

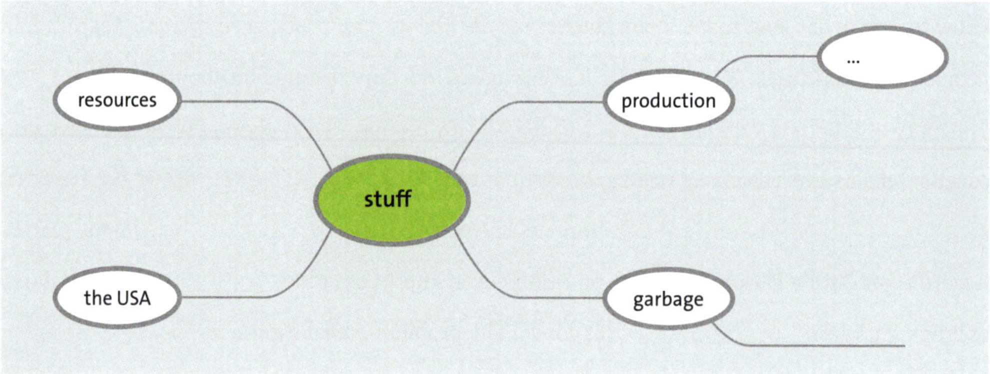

The New Pathway, p. 91

9 Food or Fuel? – The Dilemma of Eco-Fuel

GRAMMAR
Future Tenses
→ Grammar Kit, p. 211

What will the earth look like in 2100? Will mankind be able to stop pollution and generate energy in environmentally-friendly ways? Will there be enough food to feed the world's growing population?

Look into the future: Imagine you are one of the leading scientists today and you are asked to predict the future by an investigative journalist.

Use **future tenses** when talking about your predictions.

Example: There **will be** a sustainable production of crops without exploiting …
The world's population **will have doubled** but scientists **will be able** …

10 Wal-Mart of the Recycling World

The New Pathway, p. 97

Green Tech Transfer & Recycling in South Bend, Indiana, has finally managed to arouse people's interest in recycling and reuse. In this article a local journalist visits the site and interviews the owners.

Green Tech Changes Options for Reusing Waste, Avoiding Landfills

SOUTH BEND. A brisk breeze hits Michael Morris' face as he starts up a little car that will soon take him into his own world – one that's unlike any other in the area. "Hopefully you won't get a picture of us pushing it back up the hill," he says **(1)** of the electric car as he prepares to take it on a spin around the 52-acre Green Tech Park, where the new Green Tech Transfer & Recycling material recycling facility and transfer station has become all the rave.

Morris of Green Tech drives the electric car which had a bad battery on a recent trip – out of the parking lot of Green Tech's main office to begin his tour of the area. The new facility officially opened to the public on Monday.

"I think it certainly is going to be popular, Morris says **(2)** of the facility, which he touts as the first and only of its kind in the area and the only one in Indiana that handles as many commodities as it does in one place.

Mother Earth LLC is the developer for the Green Tech Transfer & Recycling facility, whose entrance is located south of Ewing Avenue and Franklin Street in the Green Tech Park. The facility's entrance road is located immediately east of the Southside Little League ball diamond near Rum Village Park.

"The $3.5 million project is expected to have a major impact on eliminating illegal dumping while, at the same time, saving tax dollars," Morris says **(3)**. "In addition to accepting regular solid waste and construction debris, Green Tech Transfer & Recycling also will accept materials such as concrete, brick, wood and other scrap and debris."

"So it's kind of the Wal-Mart of the recycling world and that was our goal," says **(4)** Morris.

"Here comes a little recycled material now," Morris says **(5)** as he travels along Green Tech Drive, where a Mack truck pulls in carrying old pieces of road from Ireland Road and Miami Street that will become recycled aggregate for driveways.

Morris turns around to follow the truck and drives up next to it, honking and smiling as the truck driver honks and smiles back. Morris knows he has good reasons to smile.

"After all, the facility," Morris says **(6)**, "is the result of 2½ years of planning and hard work."

"This is what happens when two overachievers get married, Belinda Morris chimes in with a laugh as she rides in the back seat of the electric car.

And with the construction to be completed later this summer of phase two, additional services of document destruction, paper recycling and other services will be offered, along electronic recycling – e-waste.

Plus, the Green Tech Park location – formerly the Studebaker Plant 8 manufacturing facility – is an Indiana restored Brownfield site and has been nominated for a Governor's Environmental Excellence Award Support from St. Joseph County, the city of South Bend and the Indiana Brownfields Program paved the way for the project. Morris says **(7)** he believes the facility – built with private dollars – is the first private operation that has been rebuilt on the Studebaker property. "Environmental work was done using money from the city and state," he says **(8)**.

"The facility is beneficial," Michael Morris says **(9)**, "since going to the county landfill – the closest of which is Bremen – requires a nearly 34-mile round-trip."

"To Green Tech it's about only a 14-mile round-trip from the farthest point in the city," he says **(10)**.

"This helps people save fuel amid today's rising gas prices," Morris says **(11)**. "The facility also prevents wear and tear on the roads and increases companies' productivity," he says **(12)**. "It likewise reduces people's dependence on landfills," he says **(13)**.

"On top of that, it's paving the way for local jobs and adding a tax base in the area. That includes eight to 10 jobs now and 10 to 14 jobs when the second phase is open," says **(14)** Morris. Besides that, it's just a pretty cool site to see firsthand.

"We're *inside* Studebaker Plant 8," Morris says **(15)** as he drives through an open space outside, where construction barrels are lined up and heaps of rubble lie in the distance.

He maneuvers his way through the transfer station, where a 110-yard transfer trailer is available to take certain materials to the landfill when necessary.

"Most of the materials that arrive at Green Tech are recycled and sorted, but anything that can't be used goes to the landfill," says (16) Morris, who later pulls into what's called the transfer tipping floor, where a heap of materials are all landfill-ready.

The journey continues as he drives minutes later near several stacks of Chicago common brick from the old Studebaker plant which, along with the cement blocks nearby, will be used for the new facility. Some of the Chicago common bricks will be resold to building restorers, and some are even sold to consumers who want a piece of Studebaker history.

Soon after gazing at the colorful array of bricks, Morris drives farther around the area and manages to pull up to the roof.

Wait a minute.

The *roof*?

Yes, the roof.

"This is the roof that came off the building," Morris says (17) as he points towards a heap of scraps that now sits on the ground.

"And here's what it looks like when it's done. It's dirt and chips – it's mulch," he says (18) as he points to the pile of mulch in the distance that can eventually be used for gardening and landscaping.

For Morris, it's all proof how effective recycling can be.

"After all, the 10,000-ton roof would have cost $500,000 or more to send it to a landfill," Morris says (19). "Plus, it would have used up landfill space unnecessarily," he says (20).

Today, it looks like Green Tech's philosophy has already drawn quite a few fans.

The city zoo, which brought in 400 pounds of cardboard that it had been saving up, was the first customer when Green Tech opened Monday morning. "The zoo was excited to hear about the new facility," says (21) Marcy Dean, Potawatomi Zoological Society director, who emphasizes that the zoo is a conservation organization.

"We were so fortunate, and so jumped on it, and so we took it out there – and what a great experience," Dean says (22). "Actually, we're going to be starting up a regular recycling program at the zoo now because of this."

But the zoo isn't the only one who's been eager to try out the new facility.

"Take, for instance, the guy who had taken down the wooden fence from his backyard and didn't want to put it in a landfill," Green Tech's Morris says (23). The man was at the facility even before 7 a.m. Wednesday. It's enough of an accomplishment to put a smile on Morris' face.

Of course, that isn't the only thing that puts a smile on his face.

"You didn't have to push (the car back)," he says (24) as he drives the electric car back into the main office parking lot when his tour is finished.

The battery survived today.

YaVonda Smalls, in: South Bend Tribune, May 25, 2008

COMPREHENSION

Writing Practice → FoS, Writing, p. 129

a. Divide the article into paragraphs according to their respective content, and find a suitable headline for each paragraph.

b. Using the headlines, write a summary of the newspaper article, stating what makes Green Tech so attractive and interesting for local companies and the people of South Bend.

Paraphrasing → FoL, Improving Your Style, p. 130

c. Explain and paraphrase the underlined words and phrases. If necessary, check a dictionary.

Example: (ll. 7 f.) *has become all the rave* → *The facility has become very popular and people are enthusiastic about it.*

ANALYSIS

Stylistic Devices → FoS, Analysis of a Non-Fictional Text, p. 95

d. Explain what the headline of the article implies.

e. What makes this article a local newspaper article? Find examples from the text.

GRAMMAR

Synonyms → FoL, Improving Your Style, p. 130

f. Improve the style of the text by replacing the over-used verb "say" whenever possible. In a first step, collect synonyms of the verb "say".

Examples: *speak, utter, tell, express, explain, remark, add, emphasize, reply, …*

Indirect Speech → Grammar Kit, p. 215

g. One of your friends, who didn't read the article, wants to know what the Green Tech owners explained to the reporter. Rewrite the passages in direct speech and put them into indirect speech. Be sure to use the correct tenses.

ACTIVITY

Evaluating a Text → FoS, Writing a Comment, p. 33

h. Comment on the informal tone of the article. Do you think this helps to make people interested in recycling? Give reasons for your opinion.

11 An Interview About Recycling in South Bend, Indiana

8

The New Pathway, p. 97

COMPREHENSION

Listening for Detail

→ FoS, Listening Comprehension, p. 117

a. Listen carefully to the interview with the Green Tech owner again, then say which of the answers are right or wrong. Sometimes more than one answer can be chosen.

1. Belinda Morris' motivation to start Green Tech was/were ...
   - ☐ a) her studies at Indiana University School of Public and Environmental Affairs
   - ☐ b) the 1980 Earth Day
   - ☐ c) her work with recycling buy-back centers
   - ☐ d) not mentioned in the text
2. Ms. Morris' main visions are:
   - ☐ a) to build a high-tech recycling facility in Indiana
   - ☐ b) to bring something environmentally positive to the South Bend area
   - ☐ c) leaving her community a better place than she found it
   - ☐ d) improving the health of the world
3. The old Studebaker plant is ...
   - ☐ a) perfect for a recycling facility
   - ☐ b) owned by the City of South Bend
   - ☐ c) the property of Green Tech
   - ☐ d) owned by the neighbourhood
4. Recycling the brownfield meant ...
   - ☐ a) asking the Mayor of South Bend for permission
   - ☐ b) deconstructing the buildings
   - ☐ c) convincing the neighbours of the benefits of the idea
   - ☐ d) keeping the facility as it was
5. Problems Green Tech had to tackle were ...
   - ☐ a) a complicated and long administration process
   - ☐ b) not to be held responsible and liable for environmental problems caused in the past
   - ☐ c) getting the City Council support
   - ☐ d) there weren't any serious problems at all
6. Green Tech managed to cope with the difficult situation ...
   - ☐ a) because they explored the brownfield site before, so they were able to estimate the costs
   - ☐ b) because they were given a grant from the President
   - ☐ c) because the citizens of South Bend helped to clean up the site
   - ☐ d) because people in South Bend were absolutely positive about the project and excited about such a positive development
7. What Green Tech has achieved so far ...
   - ☐ a) an operational working facility
   - ☐ b) winning an environmental award
   - ☐ c) being honoured by President Obama
   - ☐ d) not mentioned in the text
8. Belinda Morris' objectives for the future are ...
   - ☐ a) running a closed loop project and having no material landfilled
   - ☐ b) to keep on reducing the carbon footprint
   - ☐ c) building business through selling mulch and bricks
   - ☐ d) running the facility at maximum capacity

GRAMMAR
Gerund/Infinitive
→ Grammar Kit, p. 216

b. Belinda Morris stated that most importantly she wants to involve the neighbourhood in the project. Make a list of activities and events in order to address and activate the neighbours as well as the neighbouring schools. Use gerund and/or infinitive constructions.

Example: *Inviting everyone to a recycling party ...*
Teaching children how to sort trash ...

The New Pathway, p. 101

12 Municipal Waste Generation, Recycling and Disposal in the USA

ANALYSIS
Analysing Statistics
→ FoS, Analysis of Tables/Graphs/Charts, p. 163

a. Look at the pie chart and bar charts revealing the trends of waste generation and recycling in the USA.
Take notes on the questions in the box below.

Total MSW generation by material, 2007
254 million tons (before recycling)

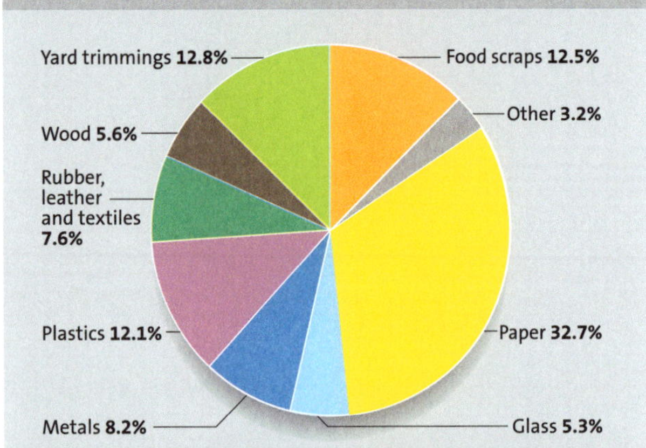

Data: EPA United States Environmental Protection Agency, Facts and Figures, 2007

Recycling rates of selected products, 2007

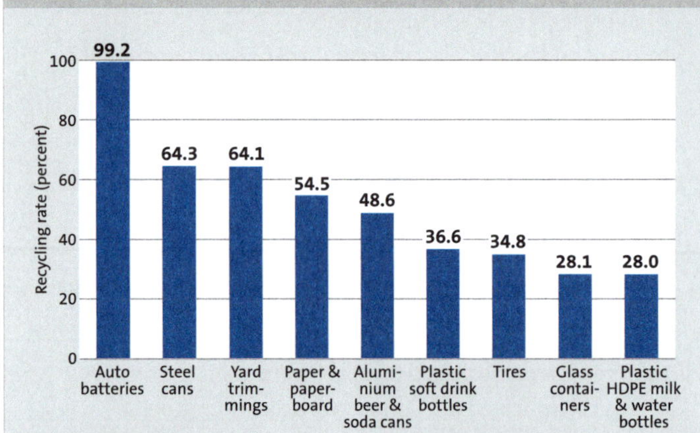

Data: EPA United States Environmental Protection Agency, Facts and Figures, 2007

1. What figures does the pie chart show – what numbers and trends do the bar charts reveal?
2. Which materials are disposed of most?
3. Make a ranking based on the numbers given in the pie chart.
4. Which are the most and least recycled products?
5. In what way do the recycling rates match the rate of waste production?
6. How has the number of landfills developed from 1988 to 2000?
   What has happened since 2000?

Number of landfills In the United States, 1988 to 2007

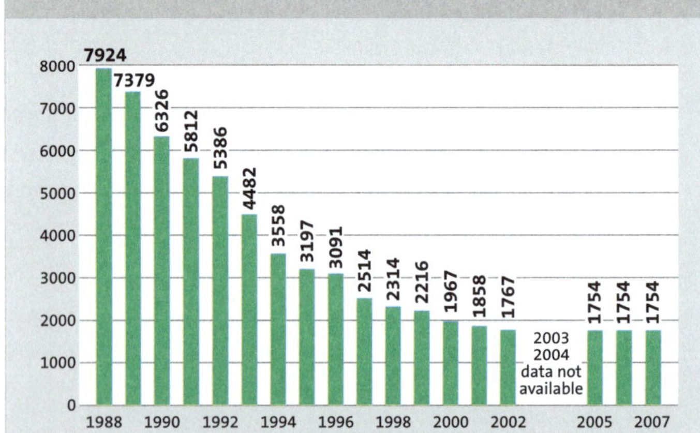

Data: EPA United States Environmental Protection Agency, Facts and Figures, 2007

b. Now, describe the pie chart and bar charts using your notes from above.

c. Think about possible reasons why the number of landfills, and most likely the recycling rates, too, have stagnated since 2000.

13 Think Global, Win Local? – Eco-Politics in Miniature

The New Pathway, p. 107

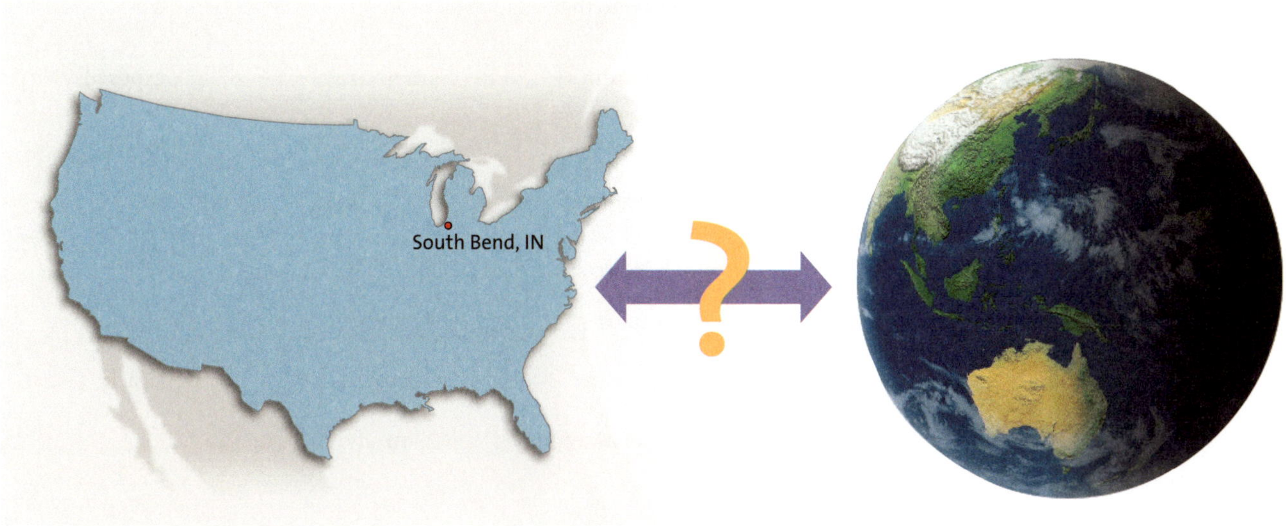

Reviewing the Green Tech success story …
Certainly this little community-based success story can serve as a role model. Which of the activities that worked out well on a local level could be successful on a national or even an international level – and which ones could not?

ACTIVITIES

Restructuring and Evaluating Information

a. Review the information about Green Tech in your Students' Book and state which of the described activities you consider promising on a wider level.

activity/strategy	South Bend	(inter-)national level
redeveloping brownfields	• Studebaker Plant 8 • …	• industrial plants • …
involving local people in the building process		
organizing neighbourhood meetings		
sorting recyclable materials		
providing work for unskilled people	• sorting old bricks • sorting mixed rubble • …	
involving students and children	• organizing fieldtrips of local high school students • …	
constructing a material recycling facility		
…		
…		

b. Based on your notes from above, work out a 3-minute presentation in which you portray the Green Tech activities and emphasize their positive effects.

Giving a Presentation
→ FoS, Presentations, p. 197

The New Pathway, p. 108

COMPREHENSION
Vocab Training

14 Focus on Vocab

Fill the respective words and phrases into the gaps.

abandoned shop	communities	green space	exposed
threaten	economy	old gas station	polluted
forgotten	contaminated	a brand new piece of land	
negative	quality	abandoned	safe
risk	employ	useful	reusing
left vacant	clean-up	created	sick
cost	to move away	empty	

Brownfields come in many shapes and sizes, from the ____________________ **(1)** that is fenced off and forgotten, to the ____________________ **(2)** which has become overgrown with weeds and falling apart. These abandoned sites may ____________________ **(3)** your health and the wellbeing of your community by polluting the soil and water around them.

Poisonous substances can make people ____________________ **(4)** if they come into contact with them, and some pollutants can even cause serious illness and death if a person is ____________________ **(5)** to them for a long time. For example, an abandoned gas station may have a leaking underground storage tank which has ____________________ **(6)** the property. It may have also ____________________ **(7)** the groundwater below with old gasoline. Scientists have discovered that some of the chemicals contained in gasoline can cause serious health problems, such as damage to the brain and the kidneys. Long-term exposure to these chemicals can even cause cancer.

Instead of providing a useful space to build another business or a home for people to live in, many old brownfields are ____________________ **(8)** because people worry about the ____________________ **(9)** of cleaning them up, or the ____________________ **(10)** of finding contamination. Also, many business people don't want to spend their money cleaning up an old property when they can buy ____________________ **(11)** that has never been used. These new areas are often called ____________________ **(12)**. As for the brownfields, they are often ____________________ **(13)**. Another serious problem related to brownfields is the ____________________ **(14)** effect that they have on the ____________________ **(15)** of life in many communities. Brownfields are not only ugly to look at, but they also pose serious problems for the local ____________________ **(16)**. A vacant property does not ____________________ **(17)** any workers, nor does it provide a safe and healthy place to live. In fact, brownfields often cause people ____________________ **(18)** from neighbourhoods. Nobody wants to live next to a building that is run-down, or open up a new business in an area where many of the shops are ____________________ **(19)** and the buildings look ______________________ **(20)**. This can lead to a snowball effect, in which an entire neighbourhood becomes run-down.

Cleaning up brownfields and turning them into __________ **(21)** and _____________ **(22)** places to work or live is becoming an increasingly popular trend across the United States, as people recognize the benefits that come with __________ **(23)** these old properties. Since 1995, the United States EPA (Environmental Protection Agency) has helped hundreds of communities by providing brownfield grants, which help to pay for the assessment, ________________ **(24)** and reuse of brownfields. Along the way, approximately 25,000 new jobs have been ___________ **(25)**. These new jobs help make families more secure during tough economic times, and this in turn helps make _______________ **(26)** stronger.

Salvaging the wreckage: Fisher Body #21 was built in 1919 to supply Cadillac and Buick. Since closing in the early 1990s, the plant has become a symbol of industrial decay. The pyramid was created by local artist Scott Hocking.

School's Out – What Next? How to Make Your Life Meaningful ...

The New Pathway, p. 110

1 Looking for Volunteers ...

Volunteer and Trainees Programs: Your dream of self-help can come true ... Help us a volunteer.

Education and knowledge is our approach to the destruction of nature.
Your action:
- Walk with us in schools and villages and teach childrens and adults the importance of protecting nature for them and their country.
- Put us to practice environmental education. The planting of trees and shrubs is an important step for the children to learn about nature.
- Through theatrical performances, video screenings, music and visits to zoo and national parks, including education about bushmeat and sustainable management of natural rainforest and the children and adults will be more closely examined.
- Even for computer-related work helping hand is always needed.
- And: Remember that things in Africa often do not always work as planned!

Discover Cameroon and contribute to the conservation welfare of people.
An unforgettable experience.

Requirements:
- Good Englisch skills and additional knowledge of French would be an advantage.
- Beside that no special knowledge is required.
- Advantage of open-mindedness and respect for other cultures, the willingness to help and to learn as well and a strong sense of humor.

All those interested in volunteer work are most welcome.

Stay:
- The minimum duration is at least 1 month, the maximum period for a stay is 3 months.
- The transfer to and from the airport is organized by WPE and is included in cost contribution.
- Working hours are from Monday to Friday. The weekend is free.
- The accommodations for our volunteers are clean but very simple.

Cost:
- The daily cost of the volunteer contribution is 25 euros per night.

a. Read the website of the Wild Planet Ecoproject (WPE) carefully and check its quality. Is there any information provided about:

- the author,
- the reputation/trustworthiness of the organization,
- recommendations of former volunteers/experts?

COMPREHENSION
Checking Websites
→ FoS, Doing Research, p. 188

b. Find out what information is given about these aspects:

activities offered	requirements	stay/accommodation	cost
• volunteer/trainees programs • education/teaching • ...	• ...	• duration: ...	• ...

c. Compare the offers made in the website above to this advert and point out the most striking differences. Think about: **layout – the reliability of the information – activities offered, etc.**

Eco-Friendly Volunteers Wanted!

Hello out there –
We are launching a revolutionary eco-friendly program here in the greater DC area soon and we need a few green-minded people to help us get the program off the ground.
We think we have a tremendous opportunity to improve our own and our neighbor's interaction with and impact on the environment.
This is not a super eco-activist movement – we're just regular people that really care about the quality of health and eco-friendliness. To that end, we have developed a program that will really resonate with lots of fellow community members (even the ones that normally don't care all that much!). If you have an interest in the environment here in our local communtity, we would love it if you would consider joining our program and volunteering a bit.
If you can send us a quick note about yourself, and maybe your zip code so that we know your general area, we will get back to you with all the information.
Thanks and hope to hear from you soon!
ourfriendlyneighborhood@web.com

d. Now, write an application to the volunteer work organisation of your choice. Your application should include all the necessary information about yourself as well as possible further questions about the institution.

e. Design your own website/advertisement in which you offer a volunteer position/a summer job/practical training (on the job), etc.

f. Briefly describe the cartoon. What are the young man's plans for his gap year in India? Comment on his understanding of "social service" – what do you think his gap year will be like?

g. Think of possible 'do's' and 'don'ts' for a gap year abroad and compare your ideas in class.

"I'm going to patronize India for my gap year, where are you going?"

ACTIVITIES
Writing Practice
→ FoS, Writing a Letter of Application, p. 122

ANALYSIS
Writing Practice
→ FoS, Writing a Comment, p. 33

The New Pathway, p. 112

2 Barack Obama: A New Era of Service 10

COMPREHENSION

Listening for Detail
→ FoS, Listening Comprehension, p. 117

a. Listen to Barack Obama's speech carefully while reading simultaneously and take notes about the aspects in the grid. Follow the structure of the text (i. e. 20 paragraphs).

paragraph/lines	contents	reference/allusion	manner of speaking	function/effect
ll. 1–10	• *daily cares and responsibilities* • *events in the world affecting the life of people*	• *influence through media* • ...		• *people feel unimportant and not responsible* • *addressing the common man*
ll. 11–18				
ll. 19–22				
ll. 23–28				
ll. 29–36				
ll. 37–45				
ll. 46–52				
ll. 53–69				
...				

ANALYSIS

Writing Practice
→ FoS, Analysis of a Political Speech, p. 116

b. Now, write an analysis of Barack Obama's speech in a coherent text.
Structure your analysis into three basic parts:

- **the introduction** (brief summary of contents, answering the w-questions)
- **the main part** (analysis of contents and structure of the speech, formal and stylistic devices as well as rhetoric)
- **a conclusion** (a final comment and evaluation of the effect/impact of the speech)

Don't forget to quote important lines/words ...!

The New Pathway, p. 112

3 A New Role Model?

In 2008 the U.S. company Jailbreak Toys launched a Barack Obama action doll. Only a short time after the presidential inauguration their new product, a Michelle Obama doll wearing the Narcisco Rodriguez dress she wore on election night, was launched very successfully.

COMPREHENSION

Collecting Arguments

a. Collect arguments for and against these trends in toy production.

for	against
• *setting positive examples for children* • ...	• *politicians are not taken seriously* • ...

ACTIVITY

Writing Practice
→ FoS, Writing a Comment, p. 33

b. Write an argumentative text of about 150 words stating whether selling these "toy politicians" or celebrities are doing any harm – or not.

4 Ask More of Us, Mr. President

The New Pathway, p. 112

In 2008, during his presidential election campaign, then-Senator Barack Obama motivated many – especially young – people to serve their country by volunteering.
Now that Obama has become president, some people expect him to be more demanding.

COMPREHENSION

Reading Comprehension
→ FoS, Reading Techniques, p. 59

a. Read the magazine article and highlight relevant information.

The Man Who Mobilized a Generation Must Now Issue Marching Orders

I watched President Obama's inauguration on my laptop, sharing a pair of earphones with a friend – one bud in my right ear, the other in her left. Like so many people, those who had voted for Obama and those who hadn't, we had great expectations that day. Never in my lifetime (I was 27) had public service had such an allure[1] (the ratio[2] of applicants to available positions in the administration was rumored[3] to be a hundred to one). Yet even as we watched the video staggering[4] over the faulty[5] wireless connection, my friend and I warned each other that our hopes for the new administration were too high.

Obama was inheriting two botched[6] wars, an amorphous[7] and ever-present terrorist threat, and the worst economic crisis in decades. It does not surprise me that we asked too much of him in his first year. What does surprise me is that Obama did not ask enough of us.

At some point in the past 30 or 40 years, politicians lost the nerve to ask much of people. I am not sure how we got from Kennedy's "ask not" to a political culture where the word "tax" has become a hex[8] but "benefit" a self-evident right. No politician wants to admit that real reform requires real sacrifice.

Obama promised to be different, and in important ways he is. He has conducted[9] himself with dignity, intelligence, and sympathy while staving off[10] another Great Depression and keeping the lid, so far, on potential eruptions around the world. He has shown us that he is a good listener and reasonable, unlike so many of his detractors[11]. But, like most politicians, he appears to assume that the public is incapable or unwilling to take on the challenges that real reform demands. [...]

Obama's younger supporters are not angry so much as disappointed. During his campaign he mobilized a generation that had been distinguished by apathy, but he has not capitalized on the energy, desire, and will of all those people who came to Washington to witness his oath of office, or who talked – as my friend and I did that day – about connecting their ambitions to the public good. Instead, we have become spectators to the appalling[12] sideshow that is Congress. [...]

We want to serve but don't know how. However impressive the numbers are in the aggregate[13], texting[14] $10 to the Red Cross seems pitifully small. Opportunities for service do exist, but they are limited or underutilized[15]. The military, the PeaceCorps, Teach for America, and such organizations and opportunities are noble callings, but viable[16] for only a few. Obama should expand and aggressively publicize FEMA's Citizen Corps, which coordinates and trains citizens in first aid and emergency skills to help communities prepare for natural disasters, terrorist attacks, crime, and other hazards. [...]

At the very least, the president should connect personal responsibility to social responsibility.

He should be honest that service isn't always heroic (taxes included). Compromise does not mean splitting the difference. It means giving up something to get something better. Obama is certainly not the first president to patronize the public. But young people are cynical because they thought he might be the first to cut through the cant[17]. He should spend less time listening to his political advisers, who are frozen by the fear of alienating[18] interest groups, and give it to us straight.

Ask more of us, Mr. President. You might be surprised by what we will give.

Louisa Thomas, in: Newsweek, February 1, 2010, p. 31

[1] **allure** the quality of being attractive and exciting – [2] **ratio** *Mengenverhältnis* – [3] **be rumored** *ein Gerücht verbreiten* – [4] **to stagger** to walk with weak unsteady steps – [5] **faulty** not perfect, defective – [6] **to botch sth. (up)** *(infml.)* to spoil sth. by doing it badly – [7] **amorphous** shapeless – [8] **hex** to use magic powers in order to harm sb. – [9] **to conduct oneself** to behave in a particular way – [10] **to stave off sth.** to prevent sth. bad from affecting you for a period of time – [11] **detractor** a person who tries to make sb./sth. seem less good by criticizing it – [12] **appalling** shocking, extremely bad – [13] **aggregate** a total number or amount made up of smaller amounts that are collected together – [14] **to text sth. to sth.** here: donate money – [15] **to be underutilized** underused – [16] **viable** that can be done – [17] **cant** hypocrisy, *Heuchelei, Scheinheiligkeit* – [18] **to alienate sb.** to make sb. less friendly or sympathetic to you

COMPREHENSION

Reading for Detail

b. Tick the correct answers. If necessary, scan the text again.

President Obama ...	Young People ...
☐ a) is different. ☐ b) is enthusiastic. ☐ c) is disappointed. ☐ d) is angry.	☐ a) are impatient. ☐ b) want to serve. ☐ c) are apathetic. ☐ d) are cynical and angry.
Volunteering organizations ...	**Politicians ...**
☐ a) should be given more donations. ☐ b) are open for everyone. ☐ c) offer great opportunities. ☐ d) help communities.	☐ a) assume people are incapable of helping. ☐ b) are afraid of alienating interest groups. ☐ c) behave appallingly in Congress. ☐ d) are good advisers to the President.
Serving your country ...	**The author wants the President ...**
☐ a) is exciting. ☐ b) is challenging. ☐ c) is a civic duty. ☐ d) demands sacrifices.	☐ a) to support the Red Cross. ☐ b) to help the military. ☐ c) to expand Citizen Corps. ☐ d) to give money to Teach for America.
The public ...	**Citizens ...**
☐ a) expects too much of President Obama. ☐ b) wants to serve the public good. ☐ c) feels socially responsible. ☐ d) wants to give more.	☐ a) should pay higher taxes. ☐ b) are expected to donate to charity. ☐ c) ought to be trained in first aid and emergency skills. ☐ d) should protest.

ANALYSIS

Language Awareness

c. Explain the underlined words and phrases. If necessary, check your dictionary.

Example: (l. 1) inauguration → *the special ceremony in which a new political leader is introduced, here: the President of the USA*

ACTIVITIES

Collecting Arguments

d. Do you agree with the author's opinion that the government should ask more of its citizens, especially young people? Collect arguments in favour of and against involving (young) people in public service.

in favour of more service	against more service
• *young people feel more accepted* • ...	• *young people should concentrate on their academic education* • ...

Writing Practice

→ FoS, Forms of Argumentative Texts, p. 95

e. Now, write a *Letter to the Editor* and state your opinion.

Start like this: *Dear Mrs. Thomas,*
I have read your essay with strong interest – but/and ...

Discussing Controversial Topics

→ FoL, Participating in a Discussion, p. 105

f. Imagine you are invited to the Oval Office to discuss volunteerism.
Write a dialogue between President Obama and young people who were/are not being accepted to do voluntary work. Point out their respective positions.
Alternatively, you can write your arguments on role cards and act out this discussion in a role play in class.

5 Bill Clinton: Hope For Haiti Now

The New Pathway, p. 112

COMPREHENSION
Reorganizing Text

On January 21, 2010 many famous politicians and international celebrities joined the *Global Benefit for Earthquake Relief* called *Hope for Haiti Now*.
Among others, former US President Bill Clinton delivered a speech that was broadcast worldwide.

a. Read the paragraphs carefully, then rearrange them so that the speech makes sense and is well-structured.

☐ Through our fund, we'll focus on helping the Haitian people to build back a better, stronger nation. Infrastructure that can withstand future disasters, better schools and higher quality education, improved health care, a more diversified[1] economy with more trade, more investment and many more good jobs – and more opportunities for an independent, clean-energy future.

☐ But it's a road we won't let the people of Haiti walk alone.

☐ I thank you for making that walk. For your support and your prayers, tonight and in the months and years to come.

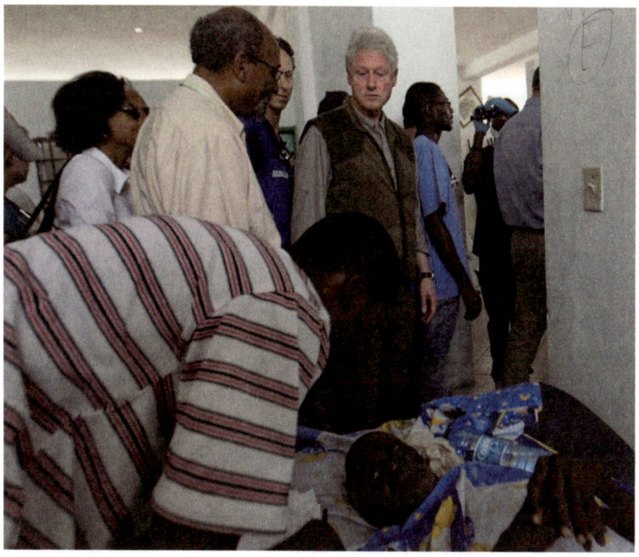

UN Special Envoy to Haiti Bill Clinton helps load supplies at the General Hospital downtown during his one visit to Haiti, Port au Prince.

1 Ever since Hillary and I took our late honeymoon trip to Haiti nearly 35 years ago, I've been totally captivated[2] by the country.
By its rich history, its culture, the beauty and bounty[3] of the land, and the amazing resilient[4] spirit of the people.

☐ Before the earthquake I already believed Haiti finally had the chance to build a stronger, more secure, more modern nation worthy of its people.
But I want you to notarize[5] that despite this tragedy I still believe they have that chance.

☐ But it will take all of us, governments and businesses and private citizens, from America and all around the world, coming together in our spirit of our common humanity to help our neighbours in need.

☐ But before we can do all that, our focus must remain on saving as many lives as possible and bringing emergency assistance to people who need it right now.
It'll be a long road of recovery[6].

☐ Last week, President Obama asked President George W. Bush and me to lead a joint fundraising effort. And I am very grateful that our *Clinton Bush Haiti Fund* will be one of the recipients of the money raised here tonight.

☐ Now, as a United Nations' envoy[7] for Haiti, I've been able to witness firsthand the great progress the Haitian people are making to overcome 200 years of poverty and oppression.

www.youtube.com/watch?v=sS48PLk_QDc [28.01.2010] (transcript of the speech by the authors)

[1] **to diversify sth.** to develop a wider range of products – [2] **to captivate** keep sb.'s attention by being interesting, attractive – [3] **bounty** generous actions – [4] **resilient** here: able to feel better quickly after sth. unpleasant such as shock, injury, etc. [5] **to notarize sth.** here: sth. that can be trusted or believed – [6] **recovery** the process of getting better – [7] **envoy** a person who represents a government and is sent as a representative to another country/ government, etc.

ANALYSIS
Stylistic Devices
→ FoS, Analysis of a Political Speech, p. 116

b. Identify the stylistic devices employed in this short speech and explain their function and effect in the chart.
In order to get a better understanding of the speech, you can watch it and listen to it at: www.youtube.com

stylistic/rhetorical device	example from the speech	function and intended effect
positive emotive word(s)	• *totally captivated*	
negative emotive word(s)		
allusions/references	• Hillary and I … late honeymoon trip	→ pattern of identification, romantic atmosphere
climax		
anti-climax		
contrast		
alliteration(s)	• *beauty and bounty …*	
anaphora		
parallelism(s)		
word groups (clusters)		
grammatical persons		
grammatical tenses		
key words/key phrases		
imagery (metaphors, personifications)		

stylistic/rhetorical device	example from the speech	function and intended effect
enumeration(s)		
language register		
numbers/factual information		
conjunctions		
...		

c. Now, after having collected the necessary details, write an analysis of the speech.

Analysing a Political Speech
→ FoS, Analysis of a Political Speech, p. 116

6 Making Dreams Come True ...

The New Pathway, p. 118

GRAMMAR

Conditional Sentences/ If-Clauses
→ Grammar Kit, p. 214

The song *If You Want to Sing Out, Sing Out* in your Students' Book suggests that (almost) everything is possible if you really believe in yourself.

Write down your dreams, wishes, and hopes for the future. Add things that you would have done differently in the past, so that the present might have turned out differently.
Use if-clauses (type I, type II and type III) for your "dreams".
Here are some examples:..

If I had saved all the money, I would have had the opportunity ...

If she loved me, I would be ...

If I pass the driving test, I will travel to ...

The New Pathway, p. 118

7 Express Yourself – Get the Life You Want

DAILY EXPRESS
THE WORLD'S GREATEST NEWSPAPER

Flying into Port-au-Prince and over Haiti is an experience I will never forget.

As I looked down I could see rows and rows of houses either collapsed, without roofs or totally destroyed. Rubble was everywhere. I was on my way to volunteer in a hospital to help the many people injured by the massive earthquake which ravaged the island on January 12 this year.

At least 150,000 people are thought to have died and I knew the situation was very serious indeed.

This wasn't my first time in a land devastated by an earthquake. Five years ago when one hit Pakistan I had my first experience of a natural disaster. I'm a plastic surgery nurse and a surgeon colleague asked me to go with him to help deal with injuries.

I had never been to Asia before and to go in those circumstances was daunting. Realising the sheer amount of people who needed help and the seriousness of the situation was hard to deal with. However, even though it was tough I was happy I could do something to help.

[...] So when I was contacted by the health charity Merlin and asked to volunteer in a hospital in Haiti I agreed immediately. I knew I was one of the only plastic surgery nurses there who had experience dealing with the aftermath of an earthquake so I hoped I'd be able to help. [...] There were many times when the aid workers, including myself, would break down in tears. The devastation to these people's lives was truly apocalyptic. On a bad day I would ring my mum and tell her about what I had seen. Phoning home and talking about my experiences made it a reality.

However, I felt guilty about crying. I was here to help and leave. I had loved ones and a home to go to. The good days came with laughter. We introduced bowling as an afternoon activity in a bid to get the patients up and out of the tents. I was worried how it would work with the mixed injuries, ages and amputees but it was great to hear people laughing.

Deleson, a young boy who was suffering from a foot infection, became the centre of attention one day. After finding out it was his 21st birthday we made it our mission to help him celebrate. We tried to replicate that for him. We sang Happy Birthday and served a birthday cake. Seeing a smile spread across Deleson's face made it all worthwhile. It was one of the happiest 21st birthday parties I've been to. I didn't volunteer in Haiti to be a hero or for any sort of personal recognition. I did it because I knew I could help people who are so much worse off than any of us are. I was just doing my job. Merlin, the charity I went with, stands for medical emergency relief for lasting health care and I hope we provided that for the Haitian people.

I was only there for 10 days and when my time came to an end I was looking forward to going home. [...] I knew the experience would be etched on my memory for a long time. The people I met were courageous, funny and inspiring. I just hoped by doing my job I had made a difference.

Sarah Finley, in: Daily Express, March 18, 2010, pp. 48 f.

Eimear (left) throwing an impromptu party. When nurse Eimear Murphy, 39, was asked to go to Haiti to work in a disaster relief hospital after the earthquake she jumped at the chance to help.

The given "interview" of the English nurse Eimear Murphy is a so-called **Human Interest Story** published in the British tabloid "Daily Express".

a. First, inform yourself about the characteristics of tabloids (Students' Book, p. 27), then read the newspaper article carefully and mark factual information and personal remarks in different colours. Briefly explain your choices.

COMPREHENSION
Distinguishing Facts from Opinion
→ FoF, The Press, p. 27

factual information	personal remarks/opinion
• *Eimear Murphy, nurse, 39* • ...	• *I felt guilty about crying ...* • ...

b. Collect examples from the text that identify this article as a human interest story. Use the characteristics given in your Students' Book and relate them to the text.

ANALYSIS
Defining Types of Newspaper
→ FoF, The Press, p. 27

characteristic	line(s)	example from the text
more sensationalist		
often one-sided/ exaggerated reporting		
no sharp line between fact and fiction/opinion		
use of subjective, often emotional or informal language	• *1 ff.* • ...	• *Flying into ... I will never forget.* • ...
...		

c. Report to a friend what Eimear Murphy reported about her stay in Haiti. Use **indirect speech**, and be sure to vary the verbs in your introductory sentence – don't always use the verb 'say'.

Start like this: *Eimear Murphy explained that flying over Haiti was an experience she would never forget. ...*

GRAMMAR
Indirect Speech
→ Grammar Kit, p. 215

d. Imagine you are a journalist working for a quality newspaper.
Rewrite the given article but change its style and characteristics. You should consider these aspects:

- Your article should be more informative and factual.
- The language should be more precise, objective and formal.
- The article should include critical comments.
- Other credible people should be quoted.

ACTIVITY
Writing Practice
→ FoS, Writing, p. 129

8 Setting Examples

The New Pathway, p. 121, No. 9

Some texts contain difficult phrases that are difficult to translate. In order to make yourself better understood, you should try to simplify these words by mediating and giving an English equivalent.

COMPREHENSION
Explaining Difficult Words
→ FoS, Mediation, p. 123

German word/expression	English equivalent
durchdachte, nonkonformistische Position	
Unangepasstheit	
Weitblick ... Zweistärkengläser	
farbenblinde, blaue Strahleaugen	
... verweigert sich dem Starrummel.	

The New Pathway, p. 125

9 Anglicisms ... Denglisch ... or Not English at All ...

Since English has become a global language we find English – or seemingly English – words in every part of life. This can be very confusing, and can lead to embarrassing misunderstandings ...

COMPREHENSION
Language Awareness

a. Complete the grid and fill in the respective words and expressions.

apparent Anglicism used in German	meaning in English	correct English word	intended German meaning
Public-viewing			öffentliche Liveübertragung eines (Sport-)ereignisses
checken	to check (inspect) sth.	• to understand • to inspect	• verstehen, begreifen • prüfen
Beamer	BMW (car)		
Ego-Shooter			Computerspiel
Handy			Mobiltelefon
roundabout			
Smoking			Abendanzug
Bodybag			Handtasche
Box			Lautsprecher
Dressman			männliches Fotomodell
Happy End			
Mobbing			
Showmaster Talkmaster			Moderator einer Talkshow
trampen			per Anhalter fahren

apparent Anglicism used in German	meaning in English	correct English word	intended German meaning
Twen			Mittzwanziger
Shooting-Star			
Streetworker			
Wellness			
catchen			ringen
kicken			
Pullunder			ärmelloser Pullover
Beauty Farm			
Service Point			Fahrkartenschalter
Spot			TV-Werbespot
Fotoshooting			
Funsport			
Oldtimer			
DJane			weiblicher Discjockey

b. Create an advertisement or leaflet for or against the use of English words in German – you may use words from the grid to illustrate your point of view.
Your text may be funny, ironic or serious. Display your adverts/leaflets in class and discuss their effect.

ACTIVITY
Creative Writing

The New Pathway, p. 126

10 Working with a Dictionary

COMPREHENSION

Language Awareness

Dictionary entries tend to be very complex because they explain many different aspects of a word or expression in a rather compressed way.

a. Answer the questions concerning the various definitions of words.

1 **vol·un·tar·ily** AW /ˈvɒləntrəli; *NAmE* ˌvɑːlənˈterəli/ *adv.* **1** willingly; without being forced: *He was not asked to leave—he went voluntarily.* **2** without payment; free: *The fund is voluntarily administered.*

→
1. Which words mean the same as *voluntarily*?
2. How many syllables does the American pronunciation have?

2 **vol·un·tary** AW /ˈvɒləntri; *NAmE* ˈvɑːlənteri/ *adj., noun*
▪ *adj.* **1** done willingly, not because you are forced: *a voluntary agreement* ◇ *Attendance on the course is purely voluntary.* ◇ *to pay* ***voluntary contributions*** *into a pension fund* ◇ (*BrE*) *He took* ***voluntary redundancy.*** OPP **compulsory** **2** [usually before noun] (of work) done by people who choose to do it without being paid: *I do some* ***voluntary work*** *at the local hospital.* ◇ *She works there on a* ***voluntary basis.*** ◇ ***voluntary services/bodies/agencies/organizations*** (= organized, controlled or supported by people who choose to do this and are usually not paid) ◇ ***the voluntary sector*** (= organizations which are set up to help people and which do not make a profit, for example charities) **3** [only before noun] (of a person) doing a job without wanting to be paid for it: *a voluntary worker* **4** (*technical*) (of movements of the body) that you can control OPP **involuntary**
▪ *noun* (*pl.* **-ies**) a piece of music played before, during or after a church service, usually on an organ

→
1. How many different meanings does the word have?
2. What are the opposites of *voluntary*?
3. What collocations are given?
4. Which of the definitions is the more commonly used one?
5. What do we learn about the position of the word in a sentence?

3 **Voluntary ˌService Overˈseas** *noun* [U] (*abbr.* **VSO**) a British charity that sends skilled people such as doctors and teachers to work in other countries as volunteers

→
1. What parts of the expression are stressed?

4 **vol·un·teer** AW /ˌvɒlənˈtɪə(r); *NAmE* ˌvɑːlənˈtɪr/ *noun, verb*
▪ *noun* **1** a person who does a job without being paid for it: *volunteer helpers* ◇ *Schools need volunteers to help children to read.* **2** a person who offers to do sth without being forced to do it: *Are there any volunteers to help clear up?* **3** a person who chooses to join the armed forces without being forced to join ➲ compare CONSCRIPT
▪ *verb* **1** [I, T] to offer to do sth without being forced to do it or without getting paid for it: **~ to do sth** *Jill volunteered to organize a petition.* ◇ **~ (for/as sth)** *Several staff members volunteered for early retirement.* ◇ **~ sth (for/as sth)** *He volunteered his services as a driver.* **2** [T] **~ sth | + speech** to suggest sth or tell sb sth without being asked: *to volunteer advice* **3** [I] **~ (for sth) | ~ to do sth** to join the army, etc. without being forced to: *to volunteer for military service* **4** [T] **~ sb (for/as sth) | ~ sb to do sth** to suggest sb for a job or an activity, even though they may not want to do it: *They volunteered me for the job of interpreter.*

→
1. What is the difference between the British and the American pronunciation of the word?
2. What type of word is *volunteer* in this entry?
3. How do the meanings of *volunteer* differ?
4. Which part of the noun is the main stress on?
5. Which of the definitions refers to informal language?

5 **the ˌVolunteer Reˈserve Forces** *noun* [pl.] the parts of the British armed forces for people who are volunteers and train in their free time so they can be used in a national emergency

→
1. What does the entry explain about the plural form of this noun?

Oxford Advanced Learner's Dictionary, 10th Edition, Oxford, Oxford University Press 2010, p. 1724

b. Say what the words and phrases mean in German.

(1) ______________________ (2) ______________________

(3) ______________________ (4) ______________________

(5) ______________________

11 Volunteering in America – American Core Values

The New Pathway, p. 126

> **"Service to others is the rent you pay for your room on earth."**
> Muhammad Ali, American boxing champion

The generosity of Americans is **true/truly (1)** something to behold. Did you know that more than 56 percent of the people of the United States are **currently/current (2)** volunteering some amount of time in the course of a year, giving an **estimated/estimatedly (3)** 19.9 billion hours? It's the highest rate of participation of any industrialized nation.

The majority volunteer on a **regularly/regular (4)** basis. And thousands more serve as full-time volunteers – whether for a summer, a year, or as their life's work.

Intrepid/Intrepidly (5), they reject the notion that things are not **possibly/possible (6)** to change. They know that to achieve progress, **voluntary/voluntarily (7)** citizen action must be applied through an organized framework. We at the Commission on Voluntary Service and Action (CVSA) describe this process as **ordinarily/ordinary (8)** people achieving **extraordinary/extraordinarily (9)** things. For **true/truly (10)** we have, and we do.

Today the **averagely/average (11)** working American labors ten to thirteen hours a day, with many of the lowest paid working ninety hours or more per week, often at multiple jobs with **diminishing/diminishingly (12)** pay. Some 45 million people in the United States have no health insurance; 35 million more are underinsured. With growing constraints on their time, many look to participate not in charities, handouts, or government-funded programs, but in **independently/independent (13)** volunteer efforts.

It's a **well/good (14)** thing they do. Worldwide, 800-plus million people are **hungry/hungrily (15)** right now. One in five of the world's people – 1.2 billion – live on less than a dollar a day. The people in more than fifty countries have lower **really/real (16)** per capita incomes today than they did a decade ago. As Americans, we have **tremendous/tremendously (17)** resources and resourcefulness within our reach. As volunteers, we have an unprecedented opportunity to advance not only the people of this country, but also those in other countries who **presently/present (18)** suffer **unimaginable/unimaginably (19)** privation.

We own a volunteer tradition stretching back to the citizens' committees of the American struggle for independence. Thousands of **independently/independent (20)** grassroots organizations, **large/largely (21)** and small, are growing and struggling, working for dignity and decency for all people throughout this nation and the world.

As a full-time volunteer working in America with these organizations and the builders who build them, and with an understanding of the conditions prevailing in the world as a **wholly/whole (22)** – I wouldn't be doing anything else anywhere else if you paid me!

Susan Angus (Executive Director Commission): Voluntary Service and Action, in: Michael Leach, I Like Being American, New York, Doubleday, 2003, pp. 110f.

GRAMMAR
Adjective/Adverb
→ Grammar Kit, p. 219

a. Read the text about the duty to serve one's country, which is considered an American core value and duty by many Americans. Think about whether to use the **adjective** or the **adverb** and cross out the incorrect alternative.

ANALYSIS
Analysing Statistical Data
→ FoS, Analysis of Tables/ Graphs/Charts, p. 163

b. The table and map offer more details on peak numbers of American volunteerism.
Compare these peak numbers on volunteering trends to the major U.S. volunteering organizations and their goals and concerns (Students' Book, p. 163).
Why might people favour this kind of work?
What do you think might be the least favourite places and ways to serve?

Regional volunteering trends

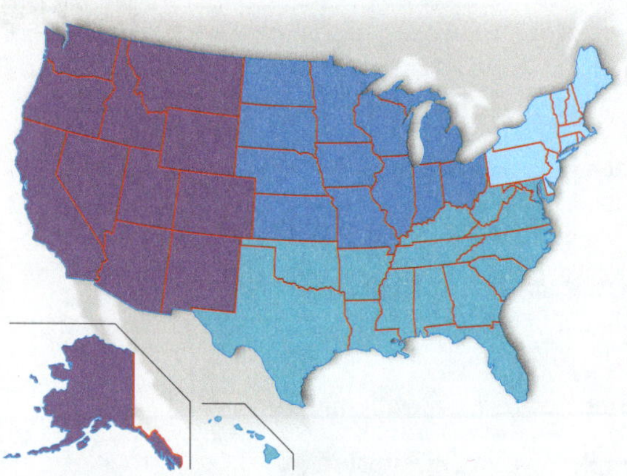

National volunteering trends

Number of volunteers	60.8 million
Volunteer rate (2007)	26.2%
Total hours volunteered	8.1 billion
Top places for people to serve	
Religious organizations	35.7%
Educational or youth service organizations	26.7%
Top volunteer activities	
Fundraise or sell items to save money	27.9%
Collect, prepare, distribute, or serve food	24.5%
Engage in general labor	21.4%
Tutor or teach	20.5%

Volunteer rates by US region (2007)

Midwest	31.1%
West	26.1%
South	24.7%
Northeast	23.4%

Data: Volunteering in America: 2008 State and City Trends and Rankings, www.VolunteeringInAmerica.gov

The New Pathway, p. 127

12 The Non-Profit Squeeze

COMPREHENSION
Scanning a Text
Collecting Arguments
→ FoS, Reading Techniques, p. 59

a. Scan the magazine article in your Students' Book on pp. 127 f. again and collect the arguments given for and against volunteer work.

arguments for volunteer work	arguments against volunteer work
• personal satisfaction • ...	• time is money • ...

ANALYSIS
Writing Practice
→ FoS, Writing a Comment, p. 33

b. Write an argumentative essay in which you juxtapose the benefits and challenges of volunteer work and compare it to the alternative of donating money to charity. Use your notes from above.

13 Responsibility Pioneers

The New Pathway, p. 127

Here are some examples of how to live meaningfully – and creatively.

Starbucks
Brewing Up Social Justice

To Starbucks, paying above-market prices for coffee beans doesn't just improve the lives of small-scale farmers. "If we build stable relationships with our growers, we'll get the highest-quality coffee," says Vivek Varma, senior VP[1] of global responsibility. The megachain recently doubled its purchase of Fair Trade coffee, to 40 million lb. (18 million kg), and wants all its coffee to be ethically sourced by 2015. Starbucks offers full health-care coverage to part-time workers too, and since October 2007, its employees have completed over 400,000 hours of community service. Good job and giving back: a rich blend!

by Sean Gregory

Embrace
High-Tech, Low-Cost Way to Save Babies

To help the millions of low-birth-weight babies born every year in the developing world many of whose mothers don't have access to electricity, let alone incubators[2] – Embrace has designed a small sleeping bag with a heating unit that, after a few minutes in boiling water, maintains a temperature of 98.6° F (37° C) for four-hour stretches. The nonprofit, founded by Stanford students, will sell the $25 warmers to health-care workers, initially in India.

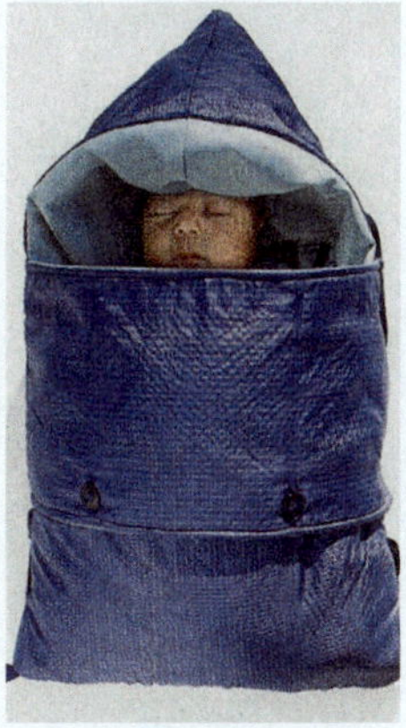

by Mridu Khullar

Better World Books
Recycled Reading

It's a beautiful system: collect unwanted books from colleges and libraries, sell them online and use some of the profits – donating about $7 million to date – to help more people (potential customers!) learn to read. Founded in 2002, Better World Books has 3 million new and used titles. Shipping is free in the U.S., but the Indiana firm charges a few cents for carbon offsets. Talk about a guilt-free read.

by Gilbert Cruz

Katie Fewings
A Bride Helps Plan Ethical Weddings

Weddings don't come cheap. Why not spend the money, Katie Fewings figured, on responsibly made products? Her 2005 nuptials in England featured fair-trade wine and a gown made locally of organic poplin. To help others find sweatshop-free dressmakers and eco-florists, she and her husband launched EthicalWeddings.com, which now draws 10,000 unique visitors a month.

by Laura Fitzpatrick

Time, September 21, 2009, pp. 32 ff.

[1] **VP** Vice President – [2] **incubator** a piece of hospital equipment into which very small and weak babies are put to keep them alive and warm

a. Skim the texts and list the needs that the people and companies are helping to meet.

COMPREHENSION

Skimming a Text
→ FoS, Reading Techniques, p. 59

b. What further needs can you think of that are not met by the social system?

ACTIVITIES

Collecting Ideas

c. Use your notes and ideas from above and design a website where you present your ideas for getting socially engaged.

Writing Practice

The New Pathway, p. 130

14 Focus on Language: Working with Phrasal Verbs

COMPREHENSION
Language Awareness

Fill in the meaning of the phrasal verb, and check your dictionary if necessary.

to back	away	move backwards in fear/dislike
	down	
	up	1)
		2)
to break	down	1)
		2) lose control of one's emotions
	into	
	out	
	out of	
	up	come to an end (e.g. marriage)
to burn	out	1)
		2) become exhausted from over-working
to call	back	
	off	
	(up)on sb.	formally invite or request
to come	across	1)
		2)
	forward	
	up against	
to cut	down on	
	out	1) remove sth. using scissors
		2)
to drop	in	
	off	1)
		2) fall asleep
	out	
to figure	out	
to hand	in	
	out	
to take	after	resemble in appearance/character
	care of	look after
	on	

	at	
	away	
	by	manage to cope/to survive
	in	
	into (+ noun)	
	off	1)
		2) remove
to get	on	
	on with sth.	
	on well with	
	out	leave
	out of (+ noun)	avoid doing sth.
	over	
	rid of	
	together	
to keep	on	
	up with	
to look	after	
	ahead	
	down on	
	for	
	forward to	
	on	be a spectator at an event
	up to	
to make	up	
to put	off	
	on	
	out	
	up	give sb. a bed, accommodate
to show	off	brag or want to be admired
	up	
to tell	off	

15 Visuals – Charity

The New Pathway, p. 131

ANALYSIS

Analysing Adverts
→ FoS, Analysis of Visuals, p. 134

a. Choose one of the posters/adverts and describe it in detail. Pay attention to colours, the eye-catching elements and the textual elements.

b. In a next step, explain what the charity is trying to do, how it will reach that goal – and how the addressee can help.

c. Compare the three adverts, stating what they have in common and what the differences are.

Tips on vocab

wooden shack ■ house built on stilts ■ dilapidated/in a state of dilapidation ■ lack of sanitation ■ to be only fit for demolition ■ unsanitary living-conditions ■ breeding ground for bacteria/germs

The New Pathway, p. 133

16 An Off Year

After a lifetime of following the rules, Cecily Powell surprises everyone by arriving for her freshman year of college ... and turning around and going home again. There are infinite possibilities for Cecily's unexpected gap year. She could volunteer, or travel around the world – but for now, Cecily is content to do absolutely nothing.

February

I had strong opinions on daytime television. *Oprah* was always good as long as it wasn't about self-improvement. Shows with more than one host were usually awful unless a guest host was sitting in. I liked Judge Mathis because he reminded me of one of my favorite teachers from grade school. But while I was a merciless critic, that didn't mean I didn't watch it all. I tried to do it on the sly, though: when Dad was out of the house, because I knew he'd get pissed if he caught me lounging on the couch watching yet another teenager screaming at an audience, "Fuck you! Y'all don't know me!"

Unfortunately, Dad came home for an early lunch one day when I was watching an episode of *Jerry Springer* that involved very fat men who enjoyed eating sloppily while not wearing many clothes.

"Oh, hi, Dad," I said, trying to keep my cool as I hastily turned off the TV.

"Nice way you spend your day," he said.

"I was just about to take Superhero for a walk," I said. Superhero, who had been lying on the floor next to me, raised his head at the *w* word. Fortunately, he couldn't speak and tell Dad he'd already been on one. [...]

March

At home, Dad and I got into a stupid fight about me going to work with him. To summarize, it went something like this: "Jane the Shrink says to ask if I can work with you a few days a week or something. I need structure and to get out of the house and to socialize."

"Good, because I was going to tell you that you needed to find a job anyway."

"Oh, you were going to *tell* me this? You were going to *make* me?" Suddenly the idea of working for my dad, which was only mildly annoying before, now seemed completely unfair. "Yes."

"What if I didn't want to work? What if I wanted to travel?"

"Well, *do* you want to travel?"

"No."

"Sometimes I don't get you, Cecily."

I shrugged. "I'm an enigma!"

He shook his head. "Don't be cute. Here's the deal. I'm not going to fund your year of sitting around doing nothing anymore. You're coming to work with me on Monday. End of story."

"Fine!" I said, and ran outside with Superhero to try to calm down and figure out what I was upset about anyway.

COMPREHENSION

Summary Writing
→ FoS, Writing, p. 129

a. The excerpts are written from a first-person narrator's point of view, which is the perspective of the protagonist, Cecily Powell.
Summarize the encounters between Cecily and her father.

ANALYSIS

b. Explain in what way the situation changes in March.

Creative Writing/ Narrative Perspective
→ FoS, Step-by-Step Analyis of a Fictional Text, p.65

c. Try to look at Cecily's lifestyle from a different perspective. Rewrite the given extracts from another point of view:

- Cecily's father's perspective as first-person narrator or
- a third-person narrator (e. g. a friend of Cecily or her dad's) who watches the situation from the outside.

d. Explain to what extent the cartoon captures the situation described in the novel.

"You don't have to worry about my future any more – I just downloaded an entire college education."

17 Starting Into the Future??

The New Pathway, p. 133

The three cartoons draw a negative and dismal picture of the future perspectives of young people finishing school.

COMPREHENSION

Working with Visuals
→ FoS, Analysis of Visuals, p. 134

a. Describe the cartoons using the words from the *Tips on vocab* boxes.

b. Sum up the gist of each cartoon in one sentence.

c. Draw your own cartoon about the future perspectives of young people today.

Graduation lemmings

Tips on vocab

graduation day ■ school-leaving qualification/high school diploma ■ ceremony where students officially receive their degrees ■ students wearing a gown and a mortar board (hat) ■ over-hanging grass/cliff ■ to fall from the edge ■ to tumble down ■ head-first ■ to be horrified at sth.

Tips on vocab

to look scared ■ a sharp contrast between ■ arrows showing in other directions ■ starting position in the middle of nowhere

Tips on vocab

to award a trophy ■ to honour sb./sb.'s achievements ■ official ceremony ■ to mock sb./sth. ■ to ridicule sb./sth.

The New Pathway, p. 133

18 Twenty-Two – One Title, Two Songs

Lily Allen
Twenty-Two (2009)

When she was 22 the future looked bright
But she's nearly 30 now and she's out every night
I see that look in her face she's got that look in her eye
She's thinking how did I get here and wondering why

It's sad but it's true how society says
Her life is already over
There's nothing to do and there's nothing to say
Till the man of her dreams comes along picks her up and puts her over his shoulder
It seems so unlikely in this day and age

She's got an alright job but it's not a career
Wherever she thinks about it, it brings her to tears
Cause all she wants is a boyfriend
She gets one-night stands
She's thinking how did I get here
I'm doing all that I can

The English singer, talk show host and actress Lily Allen

COMPREHENSION

Listening Comprehension
→ FoS, Listening Comprehension, p. 117

a. Read the lyrics and listen to the song on YouTube (www.youtube.com). Describe the woman's life and situation and the atmosphere that is created in the song.

GRAMMAR

If-Clauses
→ Grammar Kit, p. 214

b. Generally speaking, the woman's life can be divided into "before" and "after".

- First, put yourself in her position when she was 22 ... and speculate about her dreams and hopes she might have had.
  Use if-clauses (Type I) for your sentences.
  Example: *If I meet a nice boy, we will …*
- Then, imagine the woman looking back on her life and possibly regretting her decisions and dreams.
  Use if-clauses (Type III) for your sentences.
  Example: *If I had found a better job, I could have …*

Modal Auxiliaries
→ Grammar Kit, p. 220

c. The speaker of the poem wants to help her friend but doesn't know how. Therefore she asks the *Agony Aunt* of her daily newspaper for help. Now you are the agony aunt. Give advice to the woman about how she can help her friend. Use modal auxiliaries.
Start like this: *Dear Worried,*
You should be honest with your friend … You might be able to …

ACTIVITY

Writing a Comment
→ FoS, Writing a Comment, p. 33

d. Looking (critically) at the woman's dreams, comment on her wish to be carried away by the man of her dreams. Does this seem like a romantic and promising love story?

19 Twenty-Two – One Title, Two Songs

The New Pathway, p. 133

Millencolin
Twenty-Two (1997)

I'm one year older now since last time I saw you
In case you wanna know, I'm about to say what I'm up to
First of all I'm a sluggard[1] movin slow in a clumsy[2] way
Some peace of mind is what I want, but that will be the day

I've been going with the flow[3] for too long now, this must end
Running round in circles, I've been so far away from myself
Searching for the energy and the time to make a change in my life
Instead of watching it pass by, get something done while I'm alive

I'm twenty-two, don't know what I'm supposed to do
Or how to be, to get some more out of me
I'm twenty-two, so far away from all my dreams
I'm twenty-two, feeling blue

I try to activate myself the best I can
So that boredom won't catch up with me, I've got my daily plan
Wake up late, then rehearse[4] a bit with the band, I guess it's cool?
Later when I'm home again I boil a note or two
Then I go to bed that's what I do

Afraid that I will be weak forever
I can't stay in this shape any longer
My life's just another cliché

The Swedish punk rock band Millencolin, founded in 1992

[1] **sluggard** a slow, lazy person – [2] **clumsy** here: done without skill and in a way that offends people – [3] **to go with the flow** (*infml.*) to be relaxed and not worry about what one should do – [4] **to rehearse** to practice

COMPREHENSION

Listening Comprehension

a. Read the lyrics and listen to the song on YouTube (www.youtube.com). Then point out the daily routine of the speaker and the atmosphere that is created here.

ANALYSIS

Comparing Lyrics
→ FoS, Analysis of Poetry and Lyrics/Songs, p. 155

b. Compared to the other song, how is this person's situation different? Is there a (typically) male or female situation?

Language Awareness
→ FoL, The Language Register of English, p. 76

c. Examine the language register used in the two songs. What does it reveal about each person's background and/or the writers intention?

GRAMMAR

Future Tenses
→ Grammar Kit, p. 211

d. Make predictions about the future – what might the speaker of "this" poem be doing when he is thirty years old?
Use the future tense to express your ideas.

ACTIVITY

Changing the Text Form
→ FoS, Writing, p. 129

e. Choose one of the two song texts and rewrite it into a short story.
Decide on a particular point of view and add further characters if you want.
In a reading, present your various stories in class.

The New Pathway, p. 136

20 Review – Harold and Maude

Unfortunately 15 mistakes have slipped into this film review about the movie.

GRAMMAR
Spotting Mistakes

a. Underline the mistakes and correct them.

Young Harold (Bud Cort), who lives with his rich mother on their huge mansion, is insure of what to do with his life. In fact, he's more interesting in death: he drives a hearse[1], visits funerals of people which he doesn't even know, and is fond of staging his own suicide. Then he is meeting Maude (Ruth Gordon), a free spirit who will soon celebrate her 80th birthday, and she has taught him how to enjoy life. Colin Higgins scripted this touching black comedy that is something of a period piece from the last days with the hippy dream.

[...] At first the film seemed morbid, with Harold's inventible suicide games, where he pretends to hanging himself, slash his wrists[2], drown in the swimming-pool, and immolate[3] himself by fire in the manner of the news footage[4] of the Buddhist monk's self sacrifice.

As the film progresses, it has turned out that the dour[5] but innocent Harold was merely playing games on the idea of death. And then the cheerful Maude enters his life (though why she had visited funerals is never clear), a little ray of sunshine to chase away his clouds.

[...] She encourages Harold to be a individual – a lesson about a field of daisies is contrasting with the white gravestones in a war cemetery.

Graeme Clark, www.thespinningimage.co.uk/cultfilms [28.03.2010]

[1] **hearse** *Leichenwagen* – [2] **to slash one's wrists** *sich die Pulsadern aufschneiden* – [3] **to immolate** to kill sb. by burning them – [4] **news footage** *Nachrichtensendung* – [5] **dour** giving the impression of being unfriendly

ANALYSIS
Analysing a Movie Poster
→ FoS, Analysis of Visuals, p. 134

b. Describe the movie poster and say whether it captures the mood of the film.
Pay attention to details and relate them to the extract from the play and the review above.

Tips on vocab
executioner's rope ■ to flutter ■ daisies ■ police motorcycle ■ to steer (a course) ■ on the pillion seat/pillion rider ■ to tuck sth. under one's arm ■ to drive at full speed ■ exhaust pipe

21 Focus on Vocab

The New Pathway, p. 140

COMPREHENSION
Vocab Training

Complete the vocabulary list and fill in the empty boxes.

word/phrase	collocation/word field	German meaning
entrance exam(ination)	• *to take an exam*	Aufnahmeprüfung
(to) graduate		• den (Studien-) Abschluss machen/haben • ...
to apply for sth.		sich bewerben um ...
employee (*n.*)	• *employer*	
skilled (*adj.*)		
work experience		
computer literacy		EDV-Kenntnisse
after-school tutoring		Hausaufgabenbetreuung
(to) volunteer		• Freiwillige(r) • ehrenamtlich tätig sein
call to service		
gap year		
to take the opportunity	• *to grab the chance to do sth.*	
exchange student		
to study abroad		
charity (n.)		
fundraising		
to meet sb.'s basic needs		
NGO		unabhängige Hilfsorganisation
developing country		Entwicklungsland
to recruit sb.		jdn. werben/einstellen
living conditions	• *standard of living/living standards* • *the cost of living*	

Minorities in Great Britain and the USA – Redefining Race and Multi-Ethnicity

The New Pathway, p. 142

1 The Situation of Immigrants Then and Today

Heute: 23. Januar 2009
Geschafft?

Am Ende der Reise sehen sie alle irgendwie gleich aus. Dicht gedrängt sitzen sie da, lauter junge Männer, die gern Einwanderer wurden, im Identifikationszentrum der italienischen Behörden. Ihre Habseligkeiten in weißen Plastiktüten vor sich, mürrische Gesichter unter Wollmützen, der Blick geht ins Unbestimmte. Wie sollten sie auch anders schauen? Sie sind dem gelobten Kontinent so nah, sie sind gelandet, aber längst nicht angekommen. Was wird aus ihnen, jetzt, da sie es beinahe geschafft haben, über das Wasser, in winzigen Booten bis nach Lampedusa, Europas steinigem Vorposten im Mittelmeer? Dürfen sie bleiben, müssen sie zurück? Sehen sie aus, als hatten sie Durst auf ein Bier, wie Silvio Berlusconi vermutet? Oder haben sie nicht doch andere Sorgen? Jeder Mensch ist eine Insel. Und jeder sucht einen Platz in der Welt.

Damals: 1926
Geschafft!

Am Ende der Reise sehen sie alle irgendwie gleich aus. Weiße Hemden, dicke, dunkle Mantel, eine Nummer am Revers. Männer, Frauen, ein paar Kinder mit dicken Backen, die Koffer vor sich. Und ein Lächeln im Gesicht. Wie sollen sie auch anders schauen? Sie haben es beinahe geschafft, von Deutschland aus über den Atlantik bis nach Ellis Island, Amerikas Eintrittspforte im Hafen von New York, wo aus Einwanderern mit einem Federstrich Bürger werden – es sei denn, sie seien krank, Polygamisten, Prostituierte, Chinesen, Japaner oder Analphabeten. Nichts von alledem käme diesen braven Deutschen in den Sinn. Sie haben die Schatten der alten Welt hinter sich gelassen und schon einen Fuß in der Tür zur nächsten. Sie wissen nicht, was sie erwartet, aber ein Kontinent liegt vor ihnen. Kein Mensch ist eine Insel. Jeder ist eine neue Welt.

Die Zeit, 29.01.2009, Nr. 6

The two photographs show the arrival of immigrants shortly after reaching their destination.

a. Mediate the texts attached to the photographs using the words and phrases from the *Tips on vocab* boxes below.

COMPREHENSION
Mediation
→ FoS, Mediation, p. 123

2009 Tips on vocab

to look alike ■ to be exhausted ■ the rocky out-post of Europe ■ to crouch (in front of) ■ woolen caps ■ to warm oneself up ■ to be uncertain about sth. ■ to leap into the unknown ■ an uncertain future

1926 Tips on vocab

notes attached to people's clothes ■ they made it ■ to clear a hurdle ■ personal belongings ■ to be expectant/full of expectation ■ to leave sth. behind ■ to get one's foot in the door

b. Describe the photographs, pointing out the differences between the immigrants. Pay attention to details, e. g. the people's body language and facial expressions.

ANALYSIS
Describing/Analysing Visuals
→ FoS, Analysis of Visuals, p. 134

2009	1926
• *men come before the rest of their family* • *their arms crossed in front of …* • …	• *families staying together* • …

c. Think about possible reasons for these striking differences. Take into consideration the political, historical and economic conditions of each time period. Do research in your history books or on the Internet if necessary.

Doing Research
→ FoS, Doing Research, p. 188

2009	1926
• *strict/restrictive immigration policy* • *global financial crisis* • …	• *extreme unemployment rates in Germany* • *poverty due to unemployment and inflation* • …

d. Imagine you are a journalist. Choose one of the photographs and the attached text and, in a group, design the front page of a newspaper.
Collect further information (e. g. maps, statistics on immigration and/or interviews with immigrants) to present a coherent historical picture.
Display and compare your front pages in class.

ACTIVITY
Compiling a Front Page
→ FoF, The Press, p. 27

The New Pathway, p. 142

2 Global Migration in the 20th Century

The map shows the flow of voluntary migrants in the 20th century. Generally such flows have been dictated by two forces: the "push" of over-population in certain areas, and the "pull" of opportunities for work and economic advance in other areas.

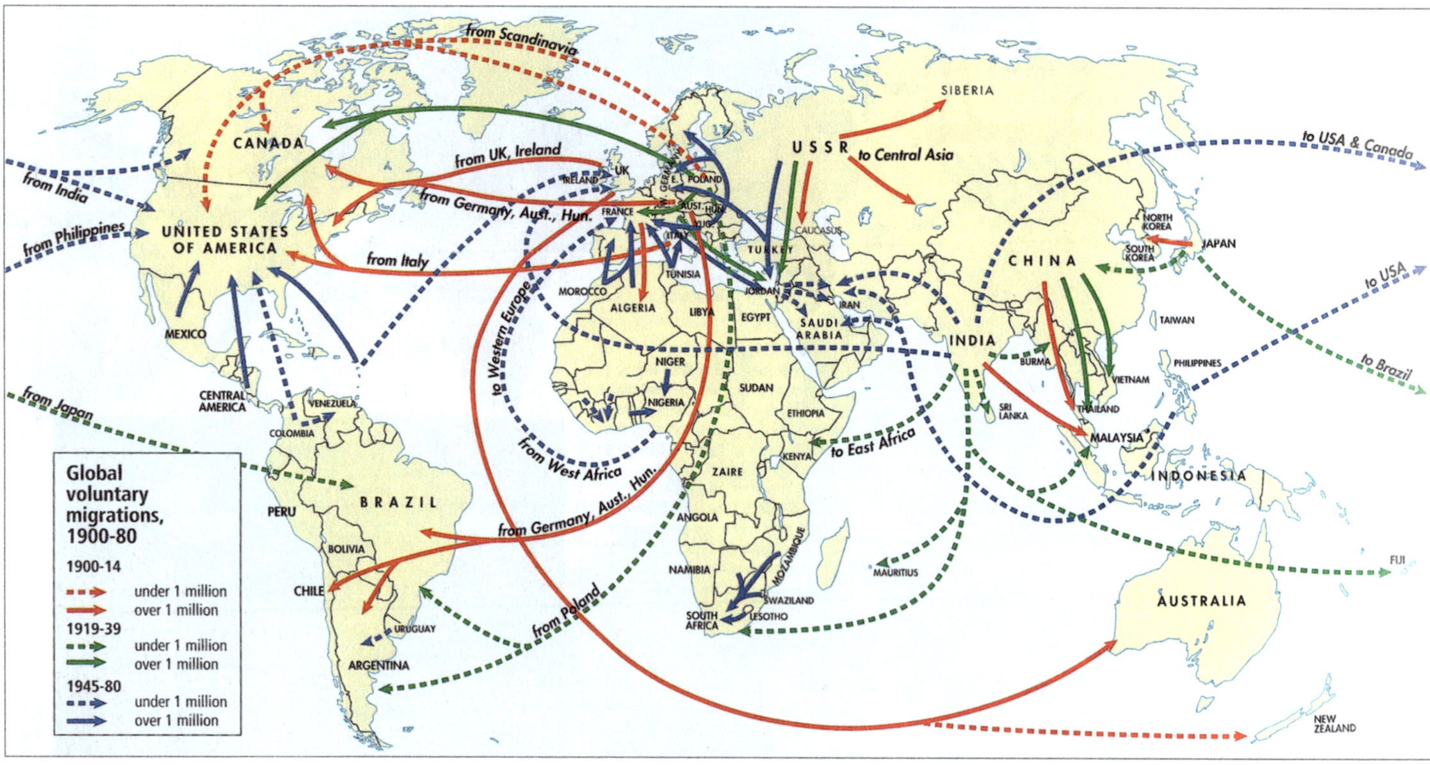

COMPREHENSION
Working with Maps

a. Give a general description of the map above and say what further details are given here compared to the maps on p. 142 in your Students' Book.

ANALYSIS
Sorting Data
→ FoS, Analysis of Tables/Graphs/Charts, p. 163

b. Fill in the information given on the waves of migration into the grid, and sort it according to historical period.

1900–1914	1919–1939	1945–1980
• pre-war years (before World War I) • ...	• ...	• the post-war years • ...

Writing Practice

c. Explain the most important flows of migration in the 20th century in a coherent text, using your notes above.

Tips on vocab

waves/streams of migrants/emigrants ■ economic refugee ■ increase in ■ reduction of ■ on a huge scale ■ in times of war ■ in times of economic crisis ■ in economically unstable times/situations

3 Using Politically Correct Language

The New Pathway, p. 144

Political Correctness

Political correctness ("PC") refers to language that deliberately avoids terms that may be considered offensive, e. g. labels regarding ethnic origin, gender or sexual orientation.
Here are some examples of politically correct expressions:

- **African-American** (in place of "Black")
- **Native American** (in place of "Indian")
- **Hispanic** (in place of "Latino" for anyone from Latin America)
- **Inuit** (in place of "Eskimo" for native people from Canada or Alaska)
- **ethnicity** (instead of "race")
- **ethnic cuisine** (instead of "foreign food")
- **undocumented immigrant** (in place of "illegal alien")

Although the expressions are meant to be polite and neutral, some terms are rather euphemistic (euphemism = a word that replaces an expression that might offend sb. or suggest sth. unpleasant, e. g. handicapped → physically challenged, death camp → concentration camp).

ACTIVITIES

Writing Practice
→ FoL, The Language Register of English, p. 76

Language Awareness
→ FoS, Writing a Comment, p. 33

a. Write a text of about 150 words about the probable ethnic background of the people shown on p. 144 in your Students' Book. Make sure to use politically correct language.

b. Comment on the use of politically correct language. What do you consider to be advantages and disadvantages? Discuss.

4 When the Ravens Were Still Colourful

The New Pathway, p. 149

comedy	tragedy	short story	film script
thriller	documentary	eco drama	sci-fi

ACTIVITY

Creative Writing
→ FoS, Writing, p. 129

a. Starting out from the headline and the two pictures given in the Students' Book, choose one of the literary genres above and write your own story.
Before you start:

- Inform yourself about the characteristics of your chosen genre.
- Collect ideas about the plot and possible characters.
- Think about a clear structure for your story.
- Think about adapting the title of the story to the genre (e. g. "Invasion of the colourful killer ravens", …).
- Organize your ideas.

The New Pathway, p. 153

5 Colonization In Reverse

Imagine if a "Colonization in Reverse" were to take place in Europe or the USA.
What do you think would happen if those countries which had been colonized in the past started to force their culture on their former colonizer instead?

ACTIVITIES
Creative Writing
→ FoS, Writing, p. 129

a. Choose one country and write a science fiction story about the possible/fictitious events that might take place. Use the information on elements of science fiction in the box below.

Elements of science fiction

- a setting in the future/in alternative timelines
- time travel
- robots/new scientific principles/innovation
- new/different political or/and social systems (e.g. organized society has collapsed ...)
- reference to environmental issues
- alternative history stories, based on the premise that historical events happened differently
- emergence of superhuman beings
- apocalyptic visions (e.g. end of civilization ...)
- comic elements/exaggerations
- dissociation (i.e. elements that are profoundly different from reality):
  - → a technological element (spaceships, time travel ...)
  - → a fantastical element (dragons, magic cell phones ...)
  - → a metaphysical element (time running backwards, effects not following causes ...)
- elements of utopia (utopian fiction = creation of an ideal world)
- elements of dystopia (dystopian fiction = creation of a nightmare world)

The New Pathway, p. 156

6 The Duty to Integrate: Shared British Values

16

COMPREHENSION
Vocab Training

Listen to the speech given by Tony Blair again and explain the following words and expressions in your own words.

ethnic minority | identity | common values | cultural difference

shared heritage | immigration | (anti-)discrimination

alienation | multi-culturalism | separation

shared values | migration | culture | integration | nationality

7 In a Generation, Minorities Will Be the U.S. Majority

The New Pathway, p. 160

Look at the chart on p. 160 of your Students' Book which makes projections of the population in the USA until 2050.

a. Using the statistical data given in this bar chart make predictions about the future development of the different ethnic groups.
Write a coherent text and use **future tenses** as well as **adverbials of time and degree** and **sentence adverbs** from the box below.

GRAMMAR
Future Tenses
Adverbs
→ Grammar Kit, pp. 211 f., 219

Example:
- *Generally*, the white non-Hispanic population *will face* a drop, from 64.7 million to ...
- *By 2040* the Hispanic population *will have risen* ...

adverbs of time	adverbs of degree	sentence adverbs
then	extremely	undoubtedly
yet	hardly	most likely
in the long run	very	probably
already	quite	generally
over time	almost	
now	completely	
in 2030 ...	considerably	
soon	totally	
in the near future	absolutely	
...	...	

b. In some of the US countries the minority-majority change has already taken place. Make detailed comparisons of the different data concerning the different ethnic groups on the map on p. 161 of your Students' Book.
Use the expressions from the box below.

Comparisons
→ FoS, Analysis of Tables/Graphs/Charts, p. 163

Example: Mitchell County in Iowa has the highest rate of ...

Tips on comparisons

more than/the most ■ less than half the population ■ fewer people than ■ the smallest number of ■ (not) as many people as ■ the difference between ■ in comparison to/compared with ■ the highest density of ... population

The New Pathway, p. 164

8 How to Date a Browngirl, Blackgirl, Whitegirl, or Halfie

Have a look at the cartoon again depicting Gustavo's life as a Hispanic immigrant on p. 167 in your Students' Book.

ANALYSIS

Analysing Statistics
→ FoS, Analysis of Tables/Graphs/Charts, p. 163

a. Compare the information on Gustavo's situation at school to the bar chart below. What are possible reasons that minority students are more afraid at school than e.g. white students? What possible fears can you think of other than being afraid of racial discrimination/prejudice? Make a list.

Percentage of students who feel afraid at school or on the way to school, by ethnicity

In general, ethnic minority students report more fear at school. However, reports of feeling afraid have declined in all groups.

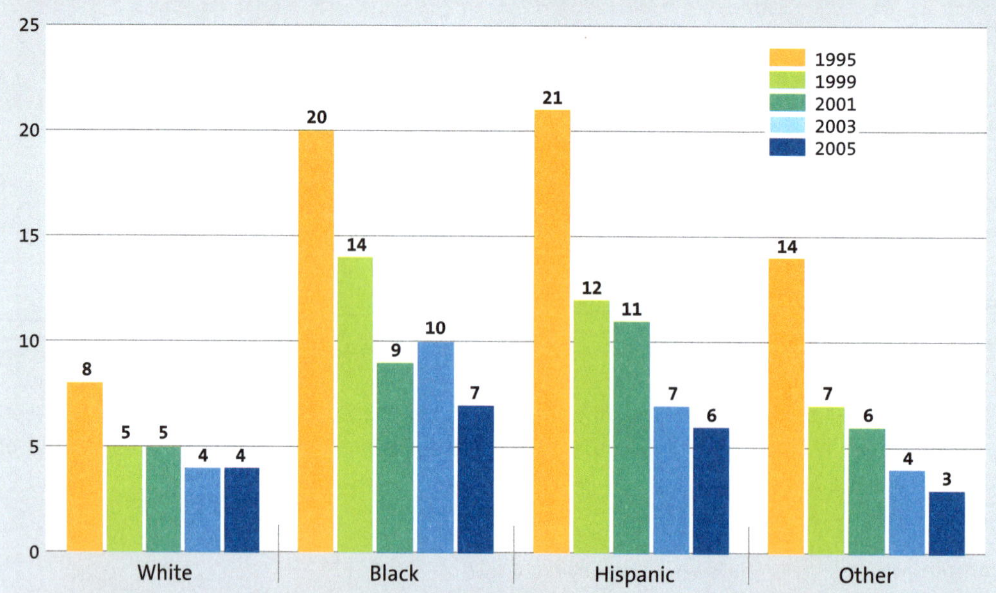

Data: National Center for Education Statistics, U.S. Department of Education, http://nces.ed.gov, 2007

ACTIVITY

Writing Practice
→ FoS, Writing, p. 129

b. Based on the cartoon in your Students' Book and the statistical data above, write a satire or fable with the title *The Perfect Immigrant*.
Your text may have a happy or sad ending – but it should have clear narrative structure.

You can start like this: *Once upon a time there was a beautiful little village in the distant country of Bolivia. There lived a poor family …*

Fable

A fable is a short narrative text in which animals represent human types or act like human beings. Fables try to teach a moral lesson and/or make a satirical comment.

Satire

A satire is a fictional text that criticizes people or certain conditions by making them appear ridiculous. This may involve exaggeration, (funny) comparisons and/or puns.

9 A Black Plum Is as Sweet as a White Plum ...

The New Pathway, p. 168

Let's take a closer look at **collocations** containing the adjective white:

white

white spirit

Whitehall

white flight

white-collar

white noise

white hope

white-knuckle ride

white lie
a harmless or small lie, esp. one that you tell to avoid hurting sb.

to white wash
an attempt to hide unpleasant facts about sb./sth. – to cover up

white knight
a person or an organization that rescues a company from being bought by another company at too low a price

white flag

white elephant

white witch

the White House

a. Look up the meaning of these collocations in your dictionary and write the explanations in the boxes above.

COMPREHENSION
Working with a Dictionary

b. Why are there so many terms that contain the adjective *white*? Explain what this implies.

ANALYSIS
Language Awareness

ACTIVITY
Cultural Awareness

c. In the next step, look up collocations containing the word *black* in your dictionary. What are (most of) these collocations associated with? Explain what impact these allusions might have for e. g. African-Americans.

The New Pathway, p. 170

10 The Namesake

Direct and Indirect Characterization

A writer can reveal the personality of a character in a direct or in an indirect way:
In a **direct characterization** the narrator or one of the other characters ***tells*** reader/audience what the personality of the respective character is like.

In an **indirect characterization** the writer ***shows/presents*** the character talking and acting which reveals the personality of the respective character.

Here are examples of **methods of indirect characterization**. The mnemonic device **STEAL** can help you to remember the basic types:

Speech	• What does the character say? • How does the character speak (choice of words, sentences, tone)? • How does the character communicate/interact with other characters?
Thoughts	• What is revealed through the character's private thoughts and feelings (e. g. in a monologue, soliloquy)?
Effect on others/ on the character	• How do other characters feel or behave in reaction to the character? • How does the character respond to other people/events? • Does the character have any relationships? Which ones?
Actions	• What does the character do? • How does the character behave (e. g. in specific situations)? → see also: body language
Looks	• What does the character look like? → appearance (hair, clothes, cleanliness ...) → body language (face, facial expression, gestures, movements, posture, physical contact ...)

ANALYSIS
Literary Characterization
→ FoS, Analysis of a Non-Fictional Text, p. 96

a. Copy the following grid into your notebook and fill in the information you find about how Gogol and his father are indirectly characterized in the text (Students' Book pp. 170 ff.).

type of indirect characterization	examples from the text	explanation of the function and effect
Speech	• *... Goggles, the name she insists on calling him instead of Dada ... (ll. 30 f.)*	• ...
Thoughts	• ...	• ...
Effect on others/ on the character	• ...	• ...
Actions	• *Gogol's ... birthday ... another excuse for his parents to throw a party for their Bengali friends (ll. 1 ff.)*	• *Gogol doesn't like these 'Bengali-style' parties* • *Gogol's parents need 'excuses' to invite their Bengali friends → are they ashamed?*
Looks	• ...	• ...

11 The Actor Kal Penn About His Role as Gogol Ganguli 18

The New Pathway, p. 174

COMPREHENSION

Listening for Detail

→ FoS, Listening Comprehension, p. 117

a. Listen carefully to the interview with Kal Penn and say which of the following statements is right. Sometimes more than one answer is possible.

1. In the film, Gogol Ganguli
   - ☐ a) is very uncomfortable with who he is.
   - ☐ b) was uncomfortable in the past but is comfortable now.
   - ☐ c) has always been very comfortable with who he is.
2. Things that prevent Gogol from sleeping at night are:
   - ☐ a) being a kid from outside New York City.
   - ☐ b) being of Indian descent.
   - ☐ c) none of these things.
3. What is Gogol's relationship with his family like?
   - ☐ a) Very close.
   - ☐ b) He ignores his family because of his girlfriend Maxine.
   - ☐ c) He doesn't want to spend much time with his father.
4. Kal Penn likes the character Gogol Ganguli because ...
   - ☐ a) they are so very different from each other.
   - ☐ b) of their similarities.
   - ☐ c) they both have a South-Asian background.
5. Kal Penn thinks that ...
   - ☐ a) films about ethnicity are great.
   - ☐ b) the audience likes films about ethnicity only when there are further universal elements.
   - ☐ c) the audience wants to learn more about the ethnic background of film characters.
6. The reason why Kal Penn likes the film character Gogol is ...
   - ☐ a) because Gogol loves acting too.
   - ☐ b) because Gogol is very passionate about what he does.
   - ☐ c) because Gogol is like Holden Caulfield in the novel *The Catcher in the Rye*.

1:04:52

1:33:37

ANALYSIS

Analysing Proverbs

b. Explain what these well-known sayings and proverbs have in common and say how they relate to cultural and/or ethnic traditions.
Do you think there is some truth in proverbs like these or in proverbs in general?

The apple never falls far from the tree.

Blood is thicker than water.

A man's home is his castle.

Custom is the guide of the ignorant.

A black hen lays white eggs.

The New Pathway, p. 175

12 Where Education and Assimilation Collide

Amalia's classes are all in English. Still, Amalia, 19, worries that because she spends most of her school day speaking Spanish with other students, and then with her parents at home, it could be years before she is able to speak, read and write English fluently enough to compete for college.

It means she has had little access to peers and networks that might help her learn to better navigate her new country, make her own MySpace page or drive a car. "If I am going to end up cleaning houses with my mother," Amalia said to explain why she almost quit Hylton, "why go to high school?"

Hylton's program, formally known as English for Speakers of other Languages, or ESOL, has become a source of pride for helping immigrant students succeed in school, but also a target of criticism that segregated classes have handicapped students by isolating them and simplifying the curriculum.

"High schools have to make a pragmatic choice when it comes to these kids," said Peter B. Bedford, a history teacher who supports the program. "Are you going to focus on educating them, or socially integrating them?"

"This school has made the choice to focus on education," he added. "The best tools we can give them to function in this society are their diplomas."

But Amy Weiler, an assistant principal, worried whether the program had turned high school into more of an end than a beginning. "If you ask whether our program is successful at getting our students to pass tests, the data would indicate that it is," Ms. Weiler said. "But if you ask whether we are helping our students to assimilate, there's no data to answer that question."

"My fear," she added, "is that if we take a look at where our ESOL students are 10 years from now, we're going to be disappointed."

Amalia, who once thought about becoming a doctor, has also learned to adjust her goals.

"When I came to this country, I had my bags packed with dreams," she said. "Now I see my dreams are limited."

Ginger Thompson, www.nytimes.com/2009/03/15/us/15immig.html [24.02.2010]

The given extract from a newspaper article emphasizes the need for immigrants to learn the language of their new country as quickly as possible.

COMPREHENSION

Reading Comprehension
→ FoS, Reading Techniques, p. 59

a. State what positive and negative consequences and what criticism of ESOL are mentioned in the text.

positive aspects	negative aspects	criticism
• helps immigrant students succeed at school • …	• learning English takes longer • hard to meet English-speaking peers • …	• isolating students • …

GRAMMAR

Relative Clauses
→ Grammar Kit, p. 217

b. Change as many sentences of the article as possible into defining or non-defining relative clauses.

Example: ll. 1ff. Amalia, whose classes are all in English, still worries …

13 Different Ways of Dealing with Immigrants

The New Pathway, p. 175

Here are some definitions of different ways of helping immigrants to adapt to the new country and new culture.

Cultural assimilation is a political response to the demographic fact of multi-ethnicity which encourages absorption of the minority into the dominant culture.
The term assimilation is often used with regard to immigrants to a new land, such as the various ethnic groups who have settled in the United States. New customs and attitudes are acquired through contact and communication. The transfer of customs is not simply a one-way process. Each group of immigrants contributes some of its own cultural traits to its new society. Assimilation usually involves a gradual change and takes place in varying degrees; full assimilation occurs when new members of a society become indistinguishable from older members.
The three-generation model of language assimilation states that the first generation makes some progress in language assimilation but remains dominant in their native tongue, the second generation is bilingual, and the third generation only speaks English.

Acculturation is the exchange of cultural customs that results when groups of individuals coming from different cultures have continuous contact living within a community.
The original cultural patterns of those groups may be altered, but the groups remain distinct, preserving their heritage. Sometimes the acculturation has irreversible impact on the preservation of the original culture, and customs and traditions get lost or are prioritized by individual groups.
Many indigenous people have mostly lost their traditional culture (most evidently language), which is replaced by that of the dominant culture.
The term is most often described as Westernization.

Social integration, in sociology and other social sciences, is the movement of minority groups such as ethnic minorities, refugees and underprivileged sections of a society into the mainstream of societies. Members of the minority groups thus gain full access to the opportunities, rights and services available to the members of the mainstream.

based on http://en.wikipedia.org [30.05.10]

COMPREHENSION
Understanding Definitions
→ FoS, Reading Techniques, p. 59

a. Point out the basic differences between the definitions given.

assimilation	acculturation	integration
• absorption into the dominant culture • …	• exchange of cultural features • …	• movement into the mainstream • …

ANALYSIS
Cultural Awareness

b. Explain the advantages and disadvantages of each adaption type.

type of adaption	advantages	disadvantages
assimilation	• transfer of customs as mutual process • …	• …
acculturation	• …	• an irreversible act • …
integration	• …	• …

The New Pathway, p. 180

14 Belonging to Different Tribes ... Explaining Metaphors

ANALYSIS

Analysing Metaphors
→ FoS, Analysis of a Fictional Text, p. 65

Junior says that he has realized that he belongs to a lot of different "tribes" (Students' Book, p. 182).

a. Fill in the grid and explain what the qualities and attitudes connected with these different "heritages" are, and what the functions of these metaphorical expressions are.

tribes of ...	related qualities and attitudes	function/connotation
Spokane Indians		
American immigrants	• *adaptability/flexibility*	
bookworms	• *interested in books/literature* • *ability to get involved in sth. new/ to focus on a fictitious character/ situation*	→ *reveals a certain cultural interest* → *reveals a certain educational level*
cartoonists	• *a sense of humour*	
chronic masturbators		
teenage boys		
small-town kids		
Pacific North-westerners		
tortilla chips-and-salsa lovers		
poverty		
funeral-goers	• *ability to show empathy/sorrow*	
beloved sons		
boys who really missed their best friends		

Text Analysis
→ FoS, Analysis of a Fictional Text, p. 65

b. Based on your findings above, write an analysis of the second part of the text (ll. 56 – 89), illustrating what "huge realizations" Junior makes.

15 Focus on Vocab

The New Pathway, p. 184

COMPREHENSION
Vocab Training

Find the corresponding nouns/adjectives/verbs and fill in the grid.

noun	adjective	verb
assimilation		
		to contribute to sth.
	discriminatory	
		to integrate
charity		
segregation		
	ethnic	———
migrant		
	restrictive	
alien		
		to civilize
exploration		
colonization		
		to expand
	invasive	
		to adapt
settlement, settler		
	———	to admit
	dominant	

Imagination and Images – Projects on Literature and Film

The New Pathway, p. 186

1 A Film Review – Real Women Have Curves

Real Women Have Curves is the story of Ana (played by America Ferrera), a Latina teenager, during the summer of her 18th year. Ana is beautiful. Hourglass figure with melon breasts, full lips and long thick hair. She's intelligent and strong-willed but is being held back by her family, especially her mother who constantly berates her because of her physical appearance. Ana lives with her family in East Los Angeles in a Mexican community but she goes to a high school in Beverly Hills; a feat she accomplished on her own. The story begins with Ana getting ready for her last day of high school. Her mother feigns being sick to get her to stay home but Ana doesn't fall for it and heads off to school showing immediately the strained relationship between these two women and the emphasis Ana places on education.

Ana's mother, Carmen (played by Lupe Ontiveros) is old school; she started working for her family when she was thirteen. She married young and became a mother. Work and family are her life. She wants the same for Ana and wants Ana to want the same which is an odd scenario because most story moms want more for their children. Carmen is needy and insults Ana about her weight in front of everyone. As the story moves on it becomes more disturbing. During her graduation party someone offers Ana some of her surprise cake and Carmen says, "Can't you see she's bigger than the cake." Despite this Ana tries to maintain a degree of self-esteem.

Carmen takes Ana to the sewing factory where she enjoys showing her the robes; unfortunately Ana purposely does badly at the job to spite her mother for not letting her go to college. She soon comes around for her sister's sake.

Estela (played by Ingrid Oliu) is Ana's adult sister. She still lives at home and runs the sewing factory where they all work, "Estela's Fashion Design." They make dresses for Bloomingdales, getting $18 a dress when the store sells them for $600. This infuriates Ana as well as the fact that they never make dresses bigger than size 7. Estela has many heavy weights beside the physical weight she carries. She's fighting to keep the factory open, pay the rent, get the dresses made on time to satisfy buyers and to keep her employees working despite the inability to pay them their wages. Three employees move back to Mexico and Estela has Ana promise to stay and help with a recent order.

With Ana's unknowing help, Estela steps outside the box and begins designing her own dresses. As a special gift, she makes a special red gown for Ana, regrettably we never get to see Ana in it. Like Ana but to a lesser degree, Carmen berates Estela. It's during one of these times Carmen mentions love, "It's because I love you that I make your life so miserable." Estela replies, "Love me less." Poignant words. [...]

George Lopez makes an appearance as Ana's teacher, Mr. Guzman. He encourages her to go to college, helps her fill out her college application and makes a special visit to plead with Ana's parents to let her go to college when she is offered a full scholarship to Columbia.

Despite this wonderful news her parents (mostly her mother) refuse to permit her to go. Ana is an adult and she could just tell her parents she's going and that's that but her mother uses the age of her grandfather to get her to stay. Although a small role, Lopez's character is effective as the nurturing teacher looking to help a woman from his own community.

The best scene in the movie is when the women in the factory strip to their underwear to expose their secrets. It all starts when Ana can't take the heat in the factory any longer and removes her shirt to cool herself. Her mother freaks, telling her she's too fat to show that much of her body. Ana is not ashamed or afraid of her body and she lets her mother know it. The other women in the factory back her up. They begin to share their body parts and how they feel about it. They take off their clothes which further infuriates Carmen. "This is who we are," yells Ana, "real women." They all celebrate each other (without Carmen) and go back to work in their underwear after Carmen walks out. This scene easily shows how Ana and Estela evolve while Carmen seems trapped in her bitterness and insecurities. She has an opportunity to bond with her

daughters, women, and chooses not to. It's very exhilarating to watch. *Real Women Have Curves* is worth watching for this scene alone.
Throughout, the movie is laced with lots of peppy Mexican music and shots of the Mexican community. [...]
I love this little film about a strong-willed girl's transition from a teenager into a woman.
[...] I would have liked Estela's storyline expanded as hers is an interesting character.
Most importantly this film's success and the success of the characters are not contingent on Ana's losing weight and finding true love to be happy. *Real Women Have Curves* is a movie not only for Latina women but, I think, for girls and women everywhere battling the views of others about how they should feel about their bodies.

M. E. Wood, in: Bella Online – The Voice of Women, www.bellaonline.com/articles/art2069.asp [10.02.2010]

COMPREHENSION
Reading Comprehension
→ FoS, Reading Techniques, p. 59

a. Read the review and take notes on Ana, Estela and Carmen.

Ana	Estela	Carmen
• Latina teenager, 17 • ...	• Ana's older sister • runs a little sewing factory • ...	• Ana and Estela's mother • ...

ANALYSIS
Reading for Detail

b. Point out what Ana and Carmen want and where their wishes clash.

c. Write down Estela's to-do list.
What do you think might make her an interesting character, as the reviewer points out?

ACTIVITIES
Working with Film Stills
→ FoF, Camera Operations, p. 21

d. Match the information given in the review to the film stills below.

1
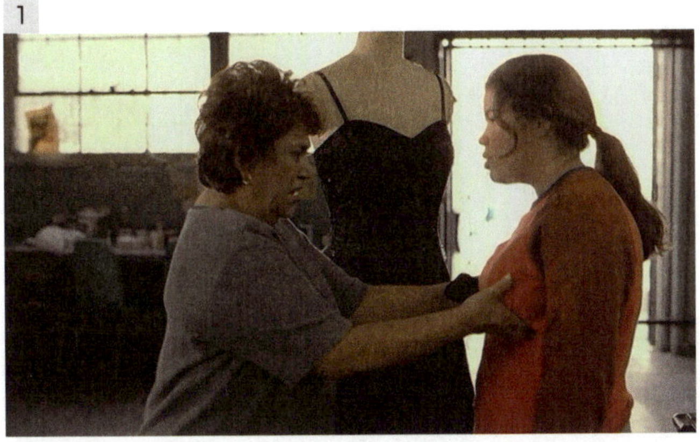
Big breasts (0:13:04)

2

Inside the sweat shop, Estela's factory (0:14:39)

3
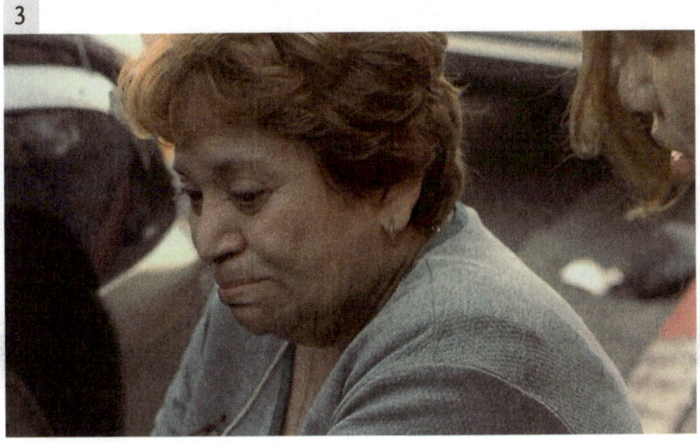
Life isn't fair – Ana and Carmen (0:19:27)

4

Writing the application (0:34:56)

5

The red dress (0:55:05)

6

A scholarship for Columbia University NYC (0:56:39)

7

Hot like hell! (1:08:03)

8

Stretch marks from north to south (1:08:55)

9

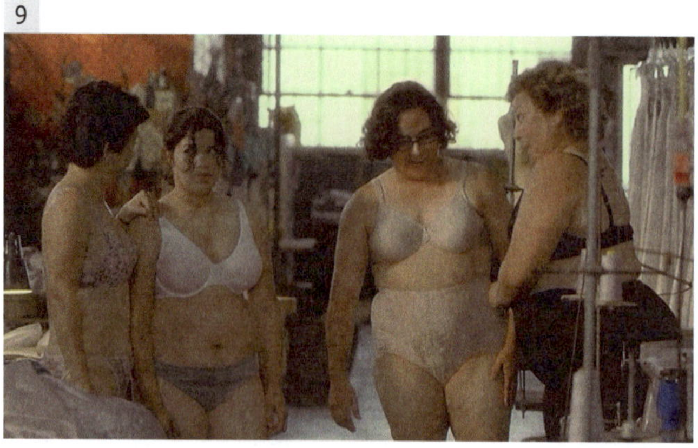

Stretch marks from east to west (1:09:09)

10

What beautiful women we are! (1:09:27)

ACTIVITY

Creative Writing

→ FoS, Writing, p. 129

e. Write dialogues and speech balloons for the film stills. Imagine what the characters might be saying to each other – or what they might be thinking.
Read out your dialogues in class.

Tip: You can copy the film stills on transparencies and read your texts like actors when they dub (= *synchronisieren*) a film. Think about possible background music or noises.

11

Ana in New York City (1:18:22)

2 Working with Film Stills – American History X

The New Pathway, p. 186

The film *American History X* tells the story of two brothers, Derek Vinyard and Daniel Vinyard, who live in Venice Beach in Los Angeles, California. Derek Vinyard is drawn into the neo-Nazi movement and kills two black gang members. He is sentenced to three years in prison. After about a year in prison, he befriends a black prison inmate, Lamont, who he is paired with in working in the prison's laundry. When his fellow neo-Nazi inmates notice this they beat and rape him in the shower.

1

1:10:11

2

1:10:17

3

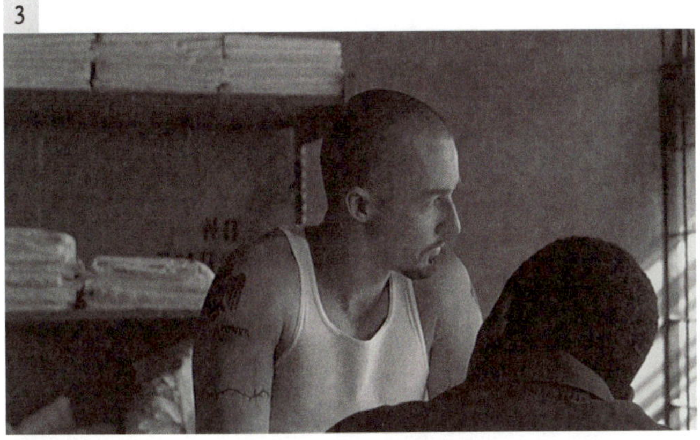

1:14:36

4

1:15:06

5

1:18:28

6

1:18:50

a. Take a close look at film stills 1–6, and pay attention to details such as props, music and the camera operations used.
Transform the film stills into a screenplay in which the action and the dialogue are described. Imagine what the characters might be saying to each other, and use the examples of screenplays given in your Students' Book (pp. 15 ff., pp. 43 ff.).

ACTIVITIES

Writing a Screenplay
→ FoF, Filmmaking, p. 23

Creative Writing
→ FoF, Filmmaking, p. 23

b. Unfortunately some of the film stills between No. 6 (1:18:50) and No. 7 (1:22:37) have been lost. Your job is to add the missing part of the story.

- What happens inbetween?
- What does the close-up hint at?
- Has Derek relapsed into his old attitude?
- Is there a further person involved?
- How has the relationship between Derek and Lamont developed/changed?

Sketch out the missing links in a storyboard.

7

1:22:37

The New Pathway, p. 193

3 The Tender Bar: Transforming Text Into Images

J.R. Moehringer
The Tender Bar

My mother and I lived in my grandfather's house, a Manhasset landmark nearly as famous as Steve's bar. People often drove by Grandpa's and pointed, and I once heard passersby speculating that the house must suffer from some sort of "painful house disease." What it really suffered from was comparisons. Set among Manhasset's elegant Gingerbread Victorians and handsome Dutch Colonials, Grandpa's dilapidated[1] Cape Cod was doubly appalling[2]. Grandpa claimed he couldn't afford repairs, but the truth was, he didn't care. With a touch of defiance[3] and a perverse pride he called his house the Shit House, and paid no attention when the roof began to sag like a circus tent. He scarcely noticed when paint peeled away in flakes the size of playing cards. [...]

Under the sagging roof my mother and I lived with Grandpa, Grandma, my mother's two grown siblings – Uncle Charlie and Aunt Ruth and Aunt Ruth's five daughters and one son. "Huddled masses yearning to breathe rent-free," Grandpa called us. While Steve was creating his public sanctuary at 550 Plandome Road, Grandpa was running a flophouse[4] at 646. Grandpa could have nailed a silhouette of Charles Dickens above his door too, since the conditions were comparable to a Dickensian workhouse. With one usable bathroom and twelve people, the waits at Grandpa's were often excruciating[5], and the cesspool[6] was constantly backed up ("Shit House" was sometimes more than a flippant nickname). The hot water ran out each morning in the middle of Shower Number Two, made a brief cameo[7] during Shower Number Three, then teased and cruelly abandoned the person taking Shower Number Four.

The furniture, much of which dated to Franklin Roosevelt's third term, was held together with duct tape and more duct tape. The only new objects in the house were the drinking glasses, "borrowed" from Dickens, and the Sears[8] living room sofa, upholstered in a hypnotically hideous pattern of Liberty Bells, bald eagles, and faces of the Founding Fathers. We called it the bicentennial sofa. We were a few years ahead of ourselves, but Grandpa said the name was right and fitting, since the sofa looked as if George Washington had used it to cross the Delaware.

The worst thing about Grandpa's house was the noise, a round-the-clock din[9] of cursing and crying and fighting and Uncle Charlie bellowing that he was trying to sleep and Aunt Ruth screaming at her six kids in the nerve-shredding key of a seagull. [...] In the House of Grandpa the heartbeat was supplied by the screen door opening and closing all day long as people came and went – *squeak bang, squeak bang* – and also by the peculiar thudding[10] way that everyone in my family walked, on their heels, like storm troopers on stilts[11]. Between the screaming and the screen door, the fighting and the stomping feet, by dusk you'd be barking and twitching more than the dog, who ran off every chance he got. But dusk[12] was the crescendo, the loudest and most tension-filled hour of the day, because dusk was dinnertime.

Seated around the lopsided dining room table, we'd talk all at once, trying to distract ourselves from the food. Grandma couldn't cook, and Grandpa gave her almost no money for groceries, so what came out of that kitchen in chipped serving bowls was both toxic and comical. To make what she called "spaghetti and meatballs", Grandma would boil a box of pasta until it was glue, saturate it with Campbell's cream of tomato soup, then top it with chunks of raw hot dog. Salt and pepper to taste. What actually brought on the indigestion, though, was Grandpa. A loner, a misanthrope, a curmudgeon[13] with a stutter[14], he found himself each night at the head of a table with twelve uninvited guests, counting the dog. A Shanty Irish reenactment of the Last Supper. As he looked us up and down we could hear him thinking, *Each of you has betrayed me tonight.* To his credit Grandpa never turned anyone away. But he never made anyone feel welcome either, and he often wished aloud that we'd all just "clear the hell out."

J.R. Moehringer: The Tender Bar. A Memoir, London, Sceptre Books, Hodder & Stoughton, 2005, pp. 15 f.

[1] **dilapidated** old and in very bad condition – [2] **appalling** shocking – [3] **defiance** *Trotz* – [4] **flophouse** (*infml.*) a cheap place to stay for people who have no home – [5] **excruciating** extremely painful or bad – [6] **cesspool** *Jauchegrube, Latrine* – [7] **cameo** here: sth. that comes back for a short time – [8] **Sears** a chain of U.S. department stores – [9] **din** a loud unpleasant noise that lasts for a long time – [10] **to thud** *stampfen* – [11] **stilt** *Stelze* – [12] **dusk** twilight – [13] **curmudgeon** badtempered person – [14] **to stutter** *stottern*

a. Read the extract from the novel carefully and divide it into paragraphs. Make notes in the margin on the topic of each paragraph.

COMPREHENSION
Reading for Detail
→ FoS, Reading Techniques, p. 59

b. Now you are the director: Hollywood has asked you to make a film of the novel *The Tender Bar*. You are asked to turn in a storyboard of the given extract as an example of your skills. Copy the grid below and work out a storyboard.

ACTIVITY
Transforming Text Into Images
→ FoF, Filmmaking, p. 23

timing	5 sec.	8 sec.	...				
image							
typical feature of the genre							
camera position	long shot of ...						
framing							
montage	cut from ...						
sound	sound of ...						

Exercise Guide

COMPREHENSION

ANALYSIS

GRAMMAR

ACTIVITIES

Acknowledgements

Illustrations

front cover: mauritius images/Marc Gilsdorf, Black Star; back cover: © Project Photos/Reinhard Eisele; p. 8: Juliet B. Schor: Born to Buy. Simon & Schuster 2005; Jacket design by Tom Brown, Jacket photograph by Frederik Broden, Copyright © 2004 Simon & Schuster Inc.; p. 11: © 2010 msnbc.com; p. 12 top: © The Sun; p. 12 bottom: taken from http://pedraenxuta.wordpress.com/2009/03/27; p. 14: © Copyright 2008 Daryl Cagle – All Rights Reserved; p. 15: Time, December 9, 1985; p. 16, 17, 38, 55: Verlagsarchiv Schöningh; p. 18: Crystal Renn with Marjorie Ingall: Hungry. Simon & Schuster 2009; Jacket design by Jackie Seow, Jacket photograph by Ruven Afanador for Simon & Schuster, Copyright © 2009 Simon & Schuster Inc.; p. 19, 32: Haderer/Stern/ Picture Press; p. 20 left: Umberto Eco: On Beauty. A History of a Western Idea. London, Secker & Warburg, 2004; p. 20 right: Umberto Eco: On Ugliness. London, Harvill Secker, 2007; p. 21 left: © Whitney Museum of American Art, New York; p. 21 right: Courtesy: Lucian Freud Archive; p. 22: photograph by Robert Maxwell; p. 24: Cinema Libre Studio; p. 25, 91: © 2006 Twentieth Century Fox Film Corporation; p. 26: © James Devaney/WireImage; p. 27: Staatsgalerie Stuttgart/ © VG Bild-Kunst, Bonn 2010; p. 28: © CARO/Andreas Teich; p. 30 top left, 30 bottom, 37 top left, 37 top right, 43 right, 44, 59, 76 bottom, 85, 86: www.CartoonStock.com; p. 30 top right: Warren; p. 35: © REUTERS/Michael Kooren; p. 36: taken from http://kotaku.com/221483/video-games-make-kids-idiots; p. 37 bottom: By Mike Smith, Las Vegas Sun, for USA Today; p. 39: Edward Winsor Kemble, illustration from the original 1884 edition of the book; p. 40: Mette/Stern/Picture Press; p. 43 left: Copyright © toonpool.com; p. 46: Matthias Stolz/Ole Häntzschel: Wofür sparen Kinder?, ZEITmagazin vom 25.2.2010; p. 47 top left: ullstein bild – Nowosti; p. 47 top right: © Panos Pictures/VISUM; p. 47 bottom left: © sinopictures/Xinhua; p. 47 bottom right: © Cultura Images RM/F1online; p. 48: photo: The Photographers, Portland, OR; p. 49: Annie Leonard: The Story of Stuff. London, Constable, 2010; p. 51: GreenTech Transfer & Recycling, LLC – South Bend, Indiana; p. 53: eathhour.org; p. 56: United States Enviromental Protection Agency; p. 57: Photograph by Sean Hemmerle; p. 58: www.ecoproject.info, © by WPE; p. 60: photo: Jailbreak Toys; p. 61: © picture-alliance/dpa; p. 63: © picture-alliance/abaca; p. 66 top: Daily Express; p. 66 bottom: © BAPRAS/Photo: James Clover; p. 71: taken from www.cvfamilycenter.org; p. 73 top left: © Starbucks; p. 73 top right: Matthew Gilson for TIME; p. 73 bottom left: Room to Read; p. 73 bottom right: Mason and Field Photography; p. 75 top left: Habitat for Humanity; p. 75 top right: World Vision Deutschland e. V.; p. 75 bottom: UN WORLD FOOD PROGRAMME (WFP); p. 76 top: Claire Zulkey: An Off-Year. New York, Dutton Books 2009; Jacket photo © 2009 by Bob Krasner, cover design by Natalie C. Sousa; p. 77 top: © Copyright 2009 Daryl Cagle – All Rights Reserved; p. 77 centre: Etta Hulme © 2004 Fort Worth Star Telegram; p. 77 bottom: © Copyright 2002 Parker – All Rights Reserved; p. 78: © action press/2VISTA; p. 79: © Naki/Redferns; p. 80: taken from www.altfg.com/blog/best-films-of/best-films-of-1971; p. 82 top: Mauro Seminara/AFP/Getty Images; p. 82 bottom: akg-images; p. 84: taken from Hammond Atlas of the 20th Century. Ed. by Richard Overy. London, Times Books 1999; p. 94: Iris Edelbrock/Verlagsarchiv Schöningh; p. 97, 98: © 2006 Alamode Film; p. 99, 100: © 2002 Universum Film

Every effort has been made to supply complete copyright information for the texts and pictures included here. Should such entries be incomplete or contain errors, we request copyright owners to contact the publishers so that we can proceed with the necessary corrections.